With Special Thanks to

THOMAS FREILING
MICHAEL KLASSEN
FEDERICO LINES

For their encouragement
and the tireless
effort of themselves
and the copy editors, typesetters,
and all the staff of
World Ahead Press

Lions, Taxes and Gold

The Prophecies of Daniel, Matthew, and Revelation Compared

William M. Fox, Th.D.

LIONS, TAXES
AND GOLD

World Ahead Press is a division of WND Books. The views and opinions expressed in this book are those of the author and do not necessarily reflect the official policy or position or WND Books.

Paperback ISBN: 978-1-944212-08-7
eBook ISBN: 978-1-944212-09-4

Printed in the United States of America
16 17 18 19 20 21 XXX 9 8 7 6 5 4 3 2 1

PREFACE

CAUTION! This book is not an easy-read book. It is a book designed to be a study guide. For that reason it has, at the beginning of each chapter, the text from God's Word, which you should read and have before you as you use this book to guide your study. You should also take the time to look up the references in the text as a guide to further understanding.

Lions, Taxes, and Gold. What in the world is this all about? The purpose of any book title is to gain attention. God's Word is directed to our attention, and many of the characters and books of God's Word have those hooks which have gained our attention and which immediately come to mind when we think of the characters or the books.

Let me ask you these questions to introduce the subject: What great prophet of God comes immediately to mind when you think of lions? What disciple of Jesus do you think of when you think of taxes? What book of the Bible do you think of when you think of the description of the streets of gold in heaven? The answer to these questions involving lions, taxes, and gold are invariably easily recognized by most church-goers as Daniel, Matthew, and Revelation. This treatise is a comparison of these three great books of the Bible, particularly the great prophetic passages of these books.

Although a great many men of God, of much greater spiritual stature and of greater renown than this writer, have written about these subjects, and have sought to impart, in many cases, a verse-by-verse exposition of these books, it has concerned this writer for many years that much of what is written has a lack of consistency in its prophetic viewpoint. There is no doubt that both Matthew and Daniel have a great deal of devotional material applicable to our everyday lives. It is also true that Matthew has a great deal of prophetic material, uttered by our Lord Himself. Certainly both Daniel and Revelation are recognized by conservative Bible scholars as prophetic books. Many times, it would seem, in attempting to make application to the daily lives of present-day saints, we lose sight of the interpretation of the prophetic outlook of these books for ourselves and for future saints of God.

It is for this reason that this study was begun. The lessons from Matthew were originally taught as part of a home Bible study series to persons of varied background and Christian experience. They were later taught from the pulpit in Sunday services, and many of the sermon illustrations are included in the writing. It has been enlarged to make comparison between Daniel and Revelation, in order that the reader may have the benefit of some of the comparisons which were made as asides in the oral presentation of these lessons.

It is the prayer and concern of the writer that as a result of the reading and perusal of this book that those who read it may, by the questions raised or the teaching given in this book, respond as the Bereans did, by searching the Scripture for themselves, so that the Holy Spirit may teach them those truths which He has for them, and that this study may be the goad which drives them to God's Word.

Real study of the Bible is a habit which is not acquired through educational courses, nor is it apt to be gained later on when the cares of a mature life and the strategy of Satan in keeping these to the fore hinder the gaining of such a blessed, power-giving, sanctifying habit in the child of God. We wrestle against Satan in the higher sphere of heavenly association ... rather than in the lower sphere of flesh and blood (Eph. 6:10–12), and few are awake to claim their deliverance from his withering touch in the most vital issues of their new life and being. A multitude of ministers must confess that they do not actually and habitually study the Bible for themselves, though they may occasionally read it for others.[1]

May God grant us grace to be diligent in the study of His Word.

ACKNOWLEDGMENTS

Dedicated to the memory of my father,
The Rev. Herbert M. Fox, with the Lord since 1987,
and to my mother, Ella M. Fox, with the Lord since 2011;
... ever the faithful teachers

IN LOVING MEMORY

of my beloved wife
Marjorie T. Fox
Taken to stand in the presence of
her Lord and Savior
July 31, 2015

CONTENTS

CHAPTER ONE

TEXT: MATTHEW 9:14–17

Whenever one begins a new class under a new professor, there is always a time of adjustment, it seems, until the student learns the ground rules under which this new professor is operating. Until such time as these are learned, it is sometimes difficult to respond to questions (particularly if they are on exams!) because you are not entirely sure what the professor wants you to say. Therefore, if it has not been done already, please leave off here and read the preface, and this will help the reader to determine one or more ground rules.

In order to help overcome that difficulty, we shall begin our study by laying down some ground rules for our study of the prophecies of Matthew, Daniel, and Revelation. Since it is of primary importance in any game to abide by the rules so that other members of the same and opposing team may understand how to play with you, we must, having adopted certain rules, be careful to abide by them. Throughout this study, the reader will be reminded to refer back to this initial chapter to refresh his or her memory on these rules. It may be that the particular terminology used by the writer may differ from that which the reader has become accustomed to, and for this reason it will be important to read this area carefully and study the terms and definitions before coming to any conclusions.

Let us then begin our study by referring to Matthew 9:14–17, with understanding that the parallel accounts are found in Mark 2:21–22, and Luke 5:36–39. The truth that we discover from this passage is that there are four principles of which the parable of the old and new wineskins and the new patch in an old garment reminds us.

The first principle is the principle of specific interpretation. By this we mean that every parable, every teaching of God's Word, has a specific direction and intent as to message, recipient, and meaning. The interpretation is discovered by study of the passage, its context, any specific interpretation which is given by the speaker or writer, and principles of interpretation which are common throughout Scripture. These parables are useful in illustrating this principle in this way. Notice that this parable is a response to a specific question posited in Matthew 9:14, "Then the disciples of John came to Him, saying, 'Why do we and the Pharisees fast, but Your disciples do not fast?' " (NASB).

The answer which Jesus gives to this question is of significance when we understand the cultural background and the fact that Jesus' answer relates directly to the question. The disciples of John ask about fasts. Jesus responds that His disciples are not in mourning (the time of fasting) but rejoicing because the Bridegroom is here (a time of feasting and celebration).

He then goes on to refer to specific customs in Jewish feasts, particularly the Passover, but also at wedding feasts, and He emphasizes two of them. First, in talking about clothing, He refers to the wearing of special garments as noted in Exodus 12:11, where the Israelites are commanded to eat the Passover clothed for travel, and He also refers to the custom outlined in Matthew 22:11, that is, the wearing of special garments at the wedding feast. Second, He refers to the custom at feasts of drinking wine at specific times during the feast. This was particularly significant in Scripture in the observance of the Passover, and Paul's reference to the "cup of blessing" in 1 Corinthians 10:16 highlights this significance.

What, then, is Jesus saying in these brief parables? He is pointing out the fact that there is a contrast between new and old. The old custom was to fast; the new is to feast in rejoicing that the Lord has come. This truth was given to Israel, the recipients of the old covenant, but ultimately was rejected by them and given as new teaching to the Gentiles. ("Let it be known to you therefore, that this salvation of God has been sent to the Gentiles; they will also listen." Acts 28:26–28 NASB). This principle of specific interpretation is very important, as we shall discuss in greater detail later, when we come to the prophecy of Daniel in Daniel 9:27, where Daniel is told, "Seventy weeks are determined upon thy people and upon thy holy city." Obviously, the question must be immediately, Who were Daniel's people, and what was his holy city, or else the interpretation of the prophecy can easily be distorted. Remember this principle of specific interpretation.

The second principle which one should recognize in any biblical study is that there is a difference between interpretation and application. As we seek the interpretation of a parable we can ask, what specific truth was Jesus, or the prophet or writer speaking through the Holy Spirit, trying to teach those who were listening, or more specifically those who "had ears to hear"? Sometimes the specific interpretation is given, as we shall see in our further studies. Other times we must compare scripture with scripture to determine what interpretation is required.

But we must further understand the principle that is so clearly stated in 2 Timothy 3:16–17, that, "All Scripture is given by inspiration of God and is profitable for doctrine, for reproof, for correction, for instruction in righteousness, that the man of God may be perfect, thoroughly furnished unto every good work." The importance of this verse is for us to be reminded that all Scripture is profitable for equipping us as saints for every good work. Its interpretation may not be specifically for us, but there will be a lesson which we can learn from it, if we allow the Holy Spirit to speak to our hearts through the Word.

With this desire and concept in mind, as we look for application of a parable, we can ask, in what circumstances were the listeners finding themselves that are like the circumstances in which I find myself? Or, what truth can I gain here which can be applied at any time in history?

For example, in these two short parables, we could realize that old is not always good. It may be for wine but not for wineskins; it may be for antique value, but not for wear and tear! We can draw from other scriptures the applications that the things of the world and spiritual things do not meld together. There are, therefore, many applications, and many lessons for our personal lives that we draw from all areas of Scripture, and yet, as in the case of many passages, we do not always apply the interpretation directly to our situation, because, quite simply, it does not fit.

Perhaps the clearest illustration of this difference between interpretation and application is to be found in the fact that evangelical Christians universally recognize the fact that the Old Testament teachings of sacrificial offerings, by interpretation, have been superseded by the perfect sacrifice of the Lord Jesus. And yet, we do not ignore the passages of Scripture which portray the sacrifices, but from them gain application of truth regarding the sins which were atoned for by them, and thus recognize the scope of the sacrifice which atones for our sins.

This leads us to the third principle, which is the principle that in order to handle accurately (2 Tim. 2:1, NASB) the Word of God, we must study interpretation as well as make application. This requires diligence in study (2 Tim. 2:15). It is relatively simple, as we have all come to realize, to make application. Often, with merely a cursory reading of Scripture, we can make a simple application to our everyday lives. This is of great importance, because it is by this means that the Holy

Spirit ministers to our need of the hour. Do not neglect applying the truth of God's Word to your heart, and, in addition, do not neglect searching for the interpretation of the passage, because it will require diligence in study, and will produce "workmen" who are not "ashamed," but who also understand and know the truth of God's Word in a way that enables them to impart it to others. Paul emphasizes this in speaking to Timothy where he says, "The things that you have heard from me, the same commit to faithful men who will be able to teach others also" (2 Tim. 2:2 NASB).

This also requires searching the Scriptures personally. Acts 17:11 records the fact that the Berean Christians "were more noble" because they "searched the Scriptures daily to see whether those things were so." May this be said of each of us; not that we have been merely spoon-fed Christians, but that we may be those who, having matured in the Christian life, are seeking the meat of God's Word in order that the application of it may not be merely a soothing balm, but may be a "sword, piercing even to the dividing asunder of joints and marrow," and a "discerner of the thoughts and intents of the heart."

It is at this point that interpretation serves to bring even greater application. As difficult as the prophecies of the book of Revelation are, it is of great encouragement to us as believers in God's Word to see what the opening verses of the book say to us. "Blessed is he that readeth, and they that hear the words of this prophecy, and keep the things which are written in it ... " (Rev 1:3). It has always been a great encouragement to know that the blessing promised from the book of Revelation is not to those who understand, but to those who read, hear, and heed! How gracious God is in understanding our weaknesses in understanding, promising blessing even when we do not understand, but are faithful to read, hear, and heed. In commenting regarding the interpretation of Scripture, Chafer says, "It is probable that, owing to human limitations, no theological system has reached that illation which is exempt from all error and which incorporates into itself all truth in its proper balance." Certainly all theologians and even church members need to be reminded of this. Chafer goes on to say:

"It is the student's task, having considered and weighed the contribution men have made to the general understanding of the Scriptures, to advance these assured results of scholarship beyond the attainments of past generations, striving to be as humble and true as the fathers have been. Among other things stated, 2 Timothy 2:15 does enjoin 'study' which is the application to, and the investigation of, the text of Scripture itself and not merely a perusal of the writings of other men about the text."[2]

The apostle Paul speaks of this principle in Romans, when having dealt with the interpretation of the rejection of the new covenant by Israel, and the "ingrafting" of the Gentile believers to the family of God, "Do not be arrogant toward the branches; but if you are arrogant, remember that it is not you who support the root, but the root supports you" (Romans

11:18 NASB). One cannot understand the application of that truth without a clear understanding and diligent searching of the interpretation of the truth that Jesus has begun to teach in the parables we are considering here, and in what Paul is therefore continuing to teach the Romans.

This principle is further emphasized in this way. In order to study interpretation within Scripture, one is required to begin to learn and recognize distinguishable facts which are consistent in Scripture and which will make the interpretation biblical, rather than heretical or cultic or apostate (2 Pet. 1:20–21 NASB). Thus, in Matthew, certain terms are important:

> 1. Kingdom of heaven – Refers most often to the Messianic rule of Christ on Earth with Israel established as the head of the nations. Will include, after its inception, believer and unbeliever and thus is not to be confused with the eternal state of the believer, which is referred to in other portions of Scripture as the Kingdom of God and the kingdom of heaven. This distinction has been questioned by many writers, but it is important to note, as you read and study the truths regarding the earthly kingdom of the Messiah, that subsequent to its inception, there will be those born who are not believers by faith in the Lord Jesus, the Messiah, and thus are not a part of the Kingdom of God, though they are, in every sense of the word, inhabitants of the kingdom of heaven. Though this concept may

not be verified at this point, watch carefully as our study progresses for this to be confirmed in the teaching of the Lord.

Please note as well, that this writer does not indicate that the term "kingdom of heaven" refers exclusively throughout Scripture, or even the book of Matthew, to the earthly reign of the Messiah. The reader will note, throughout this study, that there are times when the kingdom of heaven and the Kingdom of God are used synonymously.

There is, in this regard, a prophet of God who is often overlooked in a study of this kind, but nonetheless one who was quoted and his inspired record verified by the Lord Himself. The prophet Daniel, speaking under the inspiration of the Holy Spirit, mentions the kingdom that the God of heaven will establish, indicating that it will be a kingdom on Earth, with the "Son of Man" having dominion over "all the peoples, nations, and men of every language" (Dan. 7:14 NASB. See also Dan. 2:44). Daniel further indicates that this kingdom will be established after a "time of distress" for Israel and the interpretation given by Michael the archangel to Daniel is that Daniel's people, "your people, everyone who is found written in the book, will be rescued" (Dan. 12:1 NASB).

This concept of the kingdom of heaven, or the Messianic earthly kingdom, is clearly prophesied and taught in both Old and New Testaments.[3] Whatever term one chooses to make the distinction is of little importance, and this writer is of the conviction that much time has been spent arguing over the terms (Is the kingdom of heaven an earthly or a heavenly kingdom? Is it the same as the Kingdom of God?, etc.) rather than dealing with the clearly taught concepts of Scripture that the Lord Jesus Himself teaches in these passages in Matthew which we shall be considering.

2. Mystery – something heretofore hidden, but now revealed to the extent indicated. Perhaps the reader, like the writer, has experienced the response of those who, when inquiry was made regarding future events and the discussion of them in the Scripture, said, "[T]he secret things belong to the Lord our God" (Deut. 29:29 NASB). By this they infer that the matter of any discussion of future events is beyond the knowledge of the believer. The significant statement by the Lord is found in Matthew 13:11 when He says, "To you it has been given to know the mysteries of the kingdom of heaven ... " (NASB).

The fourth and final principle that Jesus illustrates in this short passage is the principle of continuing revelation. By this we mean that the New Testament is not written in isolation from the Old Testament. It is a continuing revelation.

What has God revealed thus far in His Word?

1   That He has chosen Israel (Gen. 12).

2   That there is a very specific time frame in God's dealing with Israel (Dan. 9:27).

3   That Israel will be dispersed and set

aside in judgment (Isa. 42:22–25), and

4 That they will be re-gathered and Christ's earthly kingdom will be established (Dan. 9; Rom. 11).

Since God has revealed these truths, and since the Old Testament teaches only the truths of the old covenant, which are now fulfilled in Christ, who has ushered in the new covenant, what will be the New Testament book, or books, which a believing remnant of Israel will use to come to an understanding of their restored relationship to the Messiah under the new covenant, and to witness to the world? Certainly Matthew is one of the key books of the New Testament in this regard for the following reasons:

1 The genealogy of Matthew 1 focuses on the Son of David, the King. Luke's genealogy focuses on the Son of Adam.

2 Matthew records the coming of the wise men, acknowledging the birth of the King. Luke records the shepherds and prophets Simeon and Anna.

3 Matthew is Jesus' affirmation of the statement of Paul in Romans 11 that God is not through with Israel.

4 Because the nation Israel will need to know certain truths of Jesus' ministry and how His kingdom will

be established, the New Testament addresses itself "to the Jew first."

Thus, both interpretation and application are of critical significance in understanding the Word of God, and in using it for our daily lives and for the equipping of others. Chafer's summary of this subject brings it to a logical conclusion when he says,

"It is exceedingly easy to twist or mold the Word of God to make it conform to one's preconceived notions. To do this is no less than 'handling the word of God deceitfully' (2 Cor. 4:2), and is worthy of judgment from Him whose Word is thus perverted. At no point may the conscience be more exercised and the mind of God more sought than when delving into the precise meaning of the Scriptures and when giving those findings to others."[4]

CHAPTER TWO

TEXT: DANIEL 2:25–45

I n our previous chapter, we introduced the premise of study of biblical prophecy and the importance of distinguishing between interpretation and application. We also discussed, briefly, the fact of God's choice of Israel as His earthly people and that there is a future for Israel. As we come to the prophetic portions of the book of Daniel, we are introduced to the fact that God is dealing with His people, Israel, but that there will be a period of time when Israel will be set aside, dispersed among the nations, and God will allow Gentile world powers to control.

In studying biblical prophecy, one must recognize the fact that since the closing of the Canon of Scripture there is prophecy which has been fulfilled, prophecy which is being fulfilled, or in the words of Revelation 1:19, "the things which are … ," and prophecy which is yet to be fulfilled, "the things which shall be hereafter." The book of Daniel falls into the category primarily of the first two—that is, prophecy which has been and is being fulfilled. As we shall see in our following chapters, the book of Revelation falls into the last two categories primarily, "the things which are and the things which shall be hereafter" (Rev. 1:19).

The prophecies of our Lord Jesus in the book of Matthew fall primarily into the final category, the prophecies of the future. In every case there are some supplemental views of past, present, and future, but these books are primarily focused in this way. For this reason, in our discussion of these books, because of this chronological order which is built in this way, our attention will not always be in all three books, but will move within the order of events as they are laid out within these prophecies in order to gain a panoramic view of these prophecies. We will begin in Daniel.

In Daniel 2:29 we read these words, spoken by Daniel to Nebuchadnezzar, "As for you, O king, while on your bed your thoughts turned to what would take place in the future ... " (NASB). Who of us has not had this happen? Nebuchadnezzar is concerned about what will happen in the future, and God in His providence begins to reveal to us, through the agency of a Gentile king, something about His plan for the future from where Nebuchadnezzar stood. For us, from our prospective, much of this is now history, and so we have the opportunity to verify the accuracy of prophetic Scripture.

Nebuchadnezzar's vision of the great image is recalled to him through God's miraculous intervention on Daniel's behalf and given its interpretation as well, so that we need not be in doubt as to its meaning and purpose. Nebuchadnezzar sees a vision of a great statue, "whose head is of gold, its breast and its arms of silver, its belly and its thighs of bronze, its legs of iron, its feet partly of iron and partly of clay" (Dan. 2:32–33). The interpretation of this vision is quite brief, without many details. Nebuchadnezzar is told that he is the head of gold, that a kingdom will follow him represented by the silver portion, another represented by the bronze portion, and another by the iron and iron-and-clay portion. In this portion of Daniel there is no further identification given other than to identify the Babylonian empire. It is clear, however—and God in His grace will provide a greater view later in the book of Daniel—that the vision is related to Nebuchadnezzar's kingdom and those kingdoms which will follow his.

Of great importance in this vision is the statement of Daniel 2:44, which says, "And in the days of those kings the God of heaven will set up a kingdom which will never be destroyed ... it will crush and put an end to all these kingdoms, but it will itself endure forever" (NASB). What does this mean? Quite clearly it speaks of a kingdom which God will establish, a permanent kingdom which will replace all preceding authority. It is prophesied to take place following the kingdoms which Nebuchadnezzar's statue represented, it will be a kingdom which will end all other kingdoms, and it will endure forever.

The statement of supreme importance for both Nebuchadnezzar and the present-day reader is this, "the great God has made known to the king what will take place in the future; so the dream is true, and its interpretation is trustworthy" (Dan. 2:45 NASB). How blessed it is to know that we have the truth and a trustworthy interpretation! The reader is not left to his or her own devices to determine what the vision means, as Nebuchadnezzar was not. God in His grace has provided the interpretation, and has added the conclusion.

But what significance does this have for us? As we continue our study, we shall look in further detail in the book of Daniel at these kingdoms and will be able to gain further knowledge about the progression of history and prophecy until we come to our present day.

For now, however, there is one truth from this chapter of Daniel which must be emphasized in order to gain perspective for future prophetic study. Nebuchadnezzar is told that "You, O king, are the king of kings, to whom the God of heaven has given the kingdom, the power, the strength, and the glory ..." (Dan. 2:37 NASB). Dr. Harry A. Ironside, commenting on this verse says that "[T]his authority was given to Nebuchadnezzar because of the rejection of Israel as God's kingdom upon earth. Had they been faithful to God, had they always been obedient to Him, royalty never would have departed from Judah."[5] He goes on to say that "because of their disobedience and manifold sins God gave their glory to the stranger, and dominion passed to the Gentiles in the person of Nebuchadnezzar."[6] Certainly this is the indication which God gives Daniel and Nebuchadnezzar in granting to Nebuchadnezzar the title of king of kings. When will this power return to God's people? When the God of heaven sets up His kingdom—at least this is the indication given at this place in God's revelation. Can this interpretation be confirmed? Let us look further. In Nebuchadnezzar's vision of the great image there are three important truths about the "times of the Gentiles."

First, the vision of Nebuchadnezzar confirms the fact that that which is unknown to men is known to God. Nebuchadnezzar had forgotten the dream and the worldly wise were not able to tell the dream and thus were unable to concoct an interpretation. Daniel is given the dream and interpretation by God as a result of prayer. An important concept that is taught here, parenthetically, is that there are certain prerequisites to true worship of God: They are commitment to ministry (Dan. 2:16), prayer for wisdom (Dan. 2:17–18), and worship, which comes only after the first two have taken place. (Dan. 2:20–23).

Second, the vision of Nebuchadnezzar confirms the biblical principle that Gentile world power is delineated only as it relates to Israel. Only those world powers are seen which are in power while Israel is in its land and worshiping at the temple. (From AD 70 this has not been the case; that is, Israel has not been in its land and worshiping at the temple – therefore U.S., British Commonwealth, etc., do not appear. The European Common Market, or its successor, may be present in the ten toes. More about this as we go on in Daniel). Remember that in Romans 11:25 Paul tells us that "blindness in part is happened to Israel until the fullness of the Gentiles be come in." James refers to this in Acts 15:14–18, where he comments that "God first concerned Himself about taking from among the Gentiles a people for His name" (NASB), and then goes on to quote the prophets Amos and Jeremiah regarding returning to "rebuild the tabernacle of David which has fallen." The entire chapter of Jeremiah 31 emphasizes this truth, and the ultimate rebuilding of Israel when he will "put My law within them, and on their heart I will write it; and I will be their God, and they shall be My people" (Jer. 31:32).

Third, the vision of Nebuchadnezzar confirms the fact that the Gentile dominion of the world is because of Israel's disobedience. God has done this in order that Israel may know that God will not be deterred from His purpose of purging Israel and ultimately bringing His people back to Him as indicated also in Jeremiah 31:27–28:

" 'Behold, days are coming,' declares the Lord, 'when I will sow the house of Israel and the house of Judah with the seed of man and with the seed of beast. And it will come about that as I have watched over them to pluck up, to break down, to overthrow, to destroy, and to bring disaster, so I will watch over them to build and to plant,' declares the Lord" (NASB).

God has also done this in order to make it clear that man cannot defeat His plan as He pointed out very clearly to Zedekiah in Jeremiah 32:5, "If you fight against the Chaldeans, you shall not succeed" (NASB).

Fourth, the vision of Nebuchadnezzar confirms the fact that the Gentile dominion of the world (and the setting aside of Israel) is in order that the gospel would come to the Gentiles. Paul makes this very clear in Romans 11:12, where he reminds us that Israel's failure is "riches for the Gentiles," and in Romans 11:22

when he describes God's dealing with Israel as "to those who fell, severity, but to you, God's kindness" (NASB). We must be aware, as we understand this principle, that the time is limited. Our job is not to try to influence the course of the world; God has that well in hand. Our job is to make known the gospel "to men that all, everywhere should repent, because He has fixed a day in which He will judge the world." (Acts 17:30–31 NASB). It is also important for us to acknowledge the fact that the course of the world's events will not be determined by Iraq, by the Russian president, by an ayatollah, or even by a president of the United States. The course of the world's events have been determined by God Himself. He is allowing the devil to deceive the nations into believing that they are in charge, but God will soon intervene directly once again. He is withholding His hand of intervention while He waits for us to make known the gospel.

The pattern for us in making known the gospel to the world s the pattern of Daniel in the interpretation of this vision. He first made a commitment to ministry—that is, he committed himself to service for God no matter what the outcome or consequences as indicated by the eighth verse of Daniel 1, "But Daniel purposed in his heart that he would not defile himself .... " After having made this commitment, when the opportunity came for ministry he took it, as indicated in Daniel 2:16 by the fact that Daniel requested time to determine the interpretation of the vision. Having made a commitment to God, he committed his life by taking the risk of committing himself to serve before he knew the outcome. Then, having taken the risk of commitment he asked for prayer for effective ministry on the part of his companions as seen in Daniel 2:18. After having received the answer from God, Daniel offered up his worship of God because of the results of the ministry. Could it be that our worship is often so empty because there has been no committed service?

CHAPTER THREE

TEXT: DANIEL 7:11–28

As the narrative of the book of Daniel has continued, Daniel has been blessed by God in providing leadership and wisdom in the capitol of the Babylonian empire. Chapter seven of Daniel takes us back, having been involved for the last several chapters in an historical narrative, Daniel now is led to record a vision which he has seen during the reign of Belshazzar, who by this time has passed from the scene.

The vision which Daniel saw is recorded for us in this chapter as the vision of four great beasts: a beast like a lion, a beast resembling a bear, a beast like a leopard, and an indescribable beast with large iron teeth and ten horns, subsequently followed by another horn which replaced three of the ten.

Much has been written about the various meanings of each of these beasts, and perhaps additional could be written. But Daniel's concern about the interpretation is focused in one particular area and thus should, no doubt, serve as a guideline for us. Note that Daniel asked regarding the "exact meaning of all this" (Dan.

7:16 NASB). As the interpretation is given, beginning in verse seventeen of Daniel chapter seven, the four beasts are described as "four kings who shall arise from the earth." Daniel does not ask further about these four kings, but desires "to know the exact meaning of the fourth beast" (Dan. 7:19 NASB). Let us then follow with Daniel, and rather than being concerned about the first three beasts, let us hear about the fourth, under the belief that what Daniel wrote at this point under the guidance of the Holy Spirit is "profitable ... for instruction in righteousness" (2 Tim. 3:16) for us, and we shall await further interpretation to know about the first three beasts.

Daniel is told that the fourth beast is a fourth kingdom on earth "which will be different from all the other kingdoms, and it will devour the whole earth and tread it down and crush it" (Dan. 7:23 NASB). He is also told that the kingdom will have ten kings, represented by the ten horns, and that three of these kings will be subdued by a "different" king, who will "speak out against the Most High and wear down the saints of the Highest One ... and they [that is the saints of the Highest One] "will be given into his hand for a time, times, and half a time" (Dan. 7:25 NASB).

An important question must be asked at this point. From Daniel's perspective, who would he think of when he thought of "saints of the Highest One"? (Dan. 7:25 NASB). Up until Daniel's time, all who came to worship God came as proselytes to Israel, to worship at the place where God had chosen to place His name, the city of Jerusalem. Those who were saints were God's people, Israel, then. God is beginning, through this prophecy, to introduce us to some important concepts regarding His future dealing with His people, Israel At least it would appear that way. We cannot equivocally state this from this portion, but certainly from Daniel's perspective, if we were in his position, we would have this inference. Can we hope for something clearer? Perhaps we can.

Not only is there reference to an individual who will seek to "wear down" (Dan. 7:25 NASB) the saints, who will intend to make alterations in times and laws, and whose kingdom and dominion is ultimately taken away, but there is also, as there was in Daniel 2, a reference to a kingdom which will be established as the kingdom of the Highest One, wherein all will serve Him. Once again, as was seen in Daniel 2 in the interpretation of Nebuchadnezzar's vision, the culmination of this vision by Daniel is the establishing of a heavenly kingdom. What has been learned thus far in Daniel about this kingdom?

1 First, this kingdom is a kingdom established by the God of heaven, the Ancient of Days (Dan. 2:44; 7:13–14).

2 Second, this kingdom destroys and replaces existing earthly kingdoms (Dan. 2:44; 7:11,14).

3 Third, this kingdom follows the events described as taking place in relation

to the previous four kingdoms (Dan. 2:44; 7:12).

There is much more to learn in relation to this kingdom, both here in the book of Daniel, where we shall spend some additional time, and then as we move on to compare the truth of Daniel with those of Matthew and Revelation.

CHAPTER FOUR

TEXT: DANIEL 8:1–27

A s in the previous chapter, we are taking a step back in time. Daniel has brought us, in the narrative, to the time of the reign of Cyrus, but in chapter seven of Daniel we returned to the second year of the reign of Belshazzar in order to know of a vision which Daniel had, as well as its interpretation.

In Daniel 8:1 we read that, "In the third year of the reign of Belshazzar the king a vision appeared to me, Daniel, subsequent to the one which appeared to me previously" (NASB). Daniel is proceeding to tell us of the visions which he had received, as a part of the interruption in his historical narrative. This vision is the vision of the ram with two horns, and the male goat with one horn, replaced by four horns, out of one of which grows another little horn.

As we progress in the chapter, Daniel, having seen the vision, "sought to understand it ..." (Dan. 8:15 NASB). The angel Gabriel is sent to tell Daniel the interpretation of the vision, and with its interpretation comes the clarification of certain details of the previous vision, as well as identification of some of the kingdoms in the vision of Nebuchadnezzar.

The ram is identified as the "kings of Media and Persia." This clarifies the bear of Daniel 7:5 and the breast and arms of silver of the image of Nebuchadnezzar in Daniel 2:32. It is interesting to note, now that the kingdom is identified clearly, that in the vision of Nebuchadnezzar there was degradation in value or quality of the kingdoms as represented by the gradation from gold to iron, though there was increase in durability and hardness or strength. This is noted in the interpretation given to Nebuchadnezzar through Daniel, which says: "After you there will arise another kingdom inferior to you ... " (Dan. 2:39 NASB). Isn't it encouraging to note that God did not miss any detail in the clarity of the details of these visions? He is not taken by surprise by the affairs of men, nor does He lack in any way in the information He has imparted to us through His Word. The lack, when we find it, is always in our inability to understand, because we are not guided by His Holy Spirit and open to the teaching of His Word.

The he-goat of Daniel 8 is then identified as the kingdom of Greece (Dan. 8:21). What struggles finite men have gone through over the years in attempting to explain how Daniel could have this information prior to the existence of the unified kingdom of Greece under Alexander the Great, but which in Daniel's time was merely a group of warring, independent states. What pains they have put themselves to in attempting to explain how this could occur, even to the extent of questioning the date of the writing of the book of Daniel, the truthfulness of the narrative, and attacking the book and labeling it as a pseudepigrapha written by one who was not really Daniel. In their opinion, the book of Daniel was nothing more than a fictionalized version of history, written after the fact. How comforting for us to read the words of our Lord Jesus in Matthew 24:15, "When you therefore shall see the Abomination of Desolation spoken of by Daniel the **prophet** ... " (emphasis mine), and to recognize that the Lord Himself confirms that Daniel was not a historian, not a writer of fictionalized history, but a prophet!

The he-goat has one large horn, initially, and that can easily be identified as Alexander the Great, the one "great" horn of the Grecian empire. Following Alexander, four kingdoms arose, "although not with his power ... " (Dan. 8:22 NASB), that is, not as a result of his influence nor of his sons' influence. These four kingdoms, historically, were given to Alexander's four generals, namely, Ptolemy, who was acknowledged as king of Egypt and the adjacent countries; Seleucus, who took Syria and Asia Minor; Lysimachus, who had the sovereignty of Thrace and the contiguous territory; and Cassander, to whom was given Macedonia and all Greece.

The four horns then pass and one little horn arises from one of them. Because of the direction in which this horn proceeds, "toward the south, toward the east, and toward the Beautiful land" (Dan. 8:9 NASB), it is apparent that it comes from the north. The Northern Kingdom of the four kings of Greece was the kingdom of Seleucus, which encompassed Syria and Asia Minor. It was from this area that Antiochus Epiphanes came, with all the atrocities of the intertestamental period. But it is also apparent, as is often the case with prophecy, that there is not only a near fulfillment of the prophecy with respect to certain details, but that the entire prophecy awaits complete fulfillment at a yet future date. Certainly, as we see the current makeup of the countries surrounding Israel, and recognize that the prophecy of Daniel 8:11, where this little horn seeks to magnify itself to be equal with the Commander of the Host, there is reason to ask more about this kingdom of the north. In which direction from Palestine does the Muslim religion find its strongholds, with its clear opposition to Israel and Judaism? The answer, in large part, is from the north, from the area of modern day Syria, Iraq, Iran, and Turkey. One could also easily ask, will this Little Horn be a future leader of the Islamic nations who opposes the nation Israel? Perhaps our continued studies will shed further light on this important question.

CHAPTER FIVE

TEXT: DANIEL 9

One of the most crucial passages in all of prophetic Scripture is before us in this chapter. The proper interpretation of this passage provides insight into much of the rest of the biblical prophetic panorama as it is unfolded in Scripture. It is of significance to the student of prophecy to record for future reference that the insight which was given to Daniel regarding the events to come were given as a direct result of his study of Scripture and recognition of his need in his own life. Daniel 9:2 indicates that Daniel read the "Word of the Lord to Jeremiah the prophet for the completion of the desolations of Jerusalem, namely, seventy years" (NASB).

Daniel knew that this time was drawing to a close, but he also acknowledged that the captivity had come because of Israel's disobedience and he acknowledged his own sin in that regard. No doubt his concern was that because of Israel's sin this timetable might be extended, and thus he prayed, that not for his own sake or the worthiness of himself or his people, but rather "for Thy sake, O Lord, let Thy face shine on Thy desolate sanctuary" (Dan. 9:17 NASB). Certainly there is a lesson here for us as we pray in Jesus' name. Is the request that we make truly on His behalf and for His name's sake, or is it for our benefit with an attached formula of prayer by which we hope it may be obtained for us? Perhaps we need to examine ourselves in the light of Daniel's prayer in order to determine if our prayers are merely "vain repetitions" (Matt. 6:7).

As Daniel was praying and confessing his sin and the sin of his people, the angel Gabriel came to him in order to "give … insight with understanding" (Dan. 9:22 NASB). The words of the angel Gabriel provide a key to all of prophetic Scripture:

> *"Seventy weeks have been decreed for your people and your holy city, to finish the transgression, to make an end of sin, to make atonement for iniquity, to bring in everlasting righteousness, to seal up vision and prophecy and to anoint the most holy place. So you are to know and discern that from the issuing of a decree to restore and rebuild Jerusalem until Messiah the Prince there will be seven weeks and sixty–two weeks; it will be built again, with plaza and moat, even in times of distress. Then after the sixty–two weeks the Messiah will be cut off and have nothing, and the people of the prince who is to come will destroy the city and the sanctuary. And its end will come with a flood; even to the end there will be war; desolations are determined. And he will make a firm covenant with the many for one week, but in the middle of the week he will put a stop to sacrifice and grain offering; and on the wing of abominations will come one who makes*

desolate, even until a complete destruction, one that is decreed, is poured out on the one who makes desolate (Dan. 9:24–27 NASB)."

There are a number of critical factors in this important statement from God's messenger. Each of them has caused some degree of argument and disagreement amongst Bible scholars (and those who claim to be Bible scholars but are skeptics), but the reader is encouraged to focus on the statements of Scripture and to follow along as we pursue the unfolding of additional related prophecies in other passages of Scripture.

First, it is important to note that the messenger says that the period of time, seventy weeks, has been decreed upon "**your** people and **your** holy city" (emphasis mine). Who was Daniel's "people"? The nation Israel, of course. What was his "holy city"? That same city to which he turned each day, three times a day, when he prayed, and for which he was cast into the den of lions (Dan. 6:10), the city of Jerusalem, to which he knew to turn because of his study of Scripture. (Remember that Solomon's prayer at the dedication of the temple had detailed these steps. When Israel is disobedient so that they are delivered into captivity, when they acknowledge their sin and confess it and return to the Lord with all their heart and "pray to Thee toward their land which Thou hast given to their fathers, the city which Thou hast chosen, and the house which I have built for Thy name; then hear their prayer and their supplication in heaven Thy dwelling place and maintain their cause, and forgive ... " (1 Kings 8:48–50 NASB). Daniel was obedient to this instruction and prayed toward the city which God had chosen, and which was also Daniel's city, the city of Jerusalem. THEREFORE, the time period of the seventy weeks, whatever that is determined to be, is related directly to Israel and Jerusalem. This is the clear statement.

Second, this period is to begin at a specific point in time, not determined by an interpreter of prophecy from human perspective, but as interpreted by God Himself and told through His messenger. The period begins with "the issuing of a decree to restore and rebuild Jerusalem" (Daniel 9:25 NASB). God, in His infinite wisdom, saw fit to establish a benchmark for the beginning of this time period which would be clear and plain to all who would accept it. The issuing of the decree, recorded in Nehemiah 2:1–8, by King Artaxerxes in 445 BC, is a decree which can be established in time by secular history as well, and in a way which God sovereignly determined by fixing the time of the decree during the lifetime of a contemporary of King Artaxerxes, none other than Herodotus, the father of modern history.[7] This is of little consequence to the student of faith, but of significance when one realizes that God chose this particular point in history so that the doubting of Israel would have no excuse.

Third, the period of the seven weeks and the sixty–two weeks, sixty–nine in all, has a definite end that can be pinpointed in Scripture and secular history. It is defined in the passage before us as continuing "until Messiah the Prince" and after which time "the Messiah will be cut off" (Daniel 9:25–26). When did this occur?

In responding to this it is important to understand the seeming misnomer which occurs in the language. We who speak English think of the term "Messiah" as a name for the Lord Jesus, and it is; but it would be clearer to us if it were translated "king." When would we, under circumstances which we could envision, speak of the king, the prince? Probably, as we spoke of one who was being presented as the king, who was rightful heir to the throne, who had received authority from the sovereign (retiring or dying in the human realm, normally) to be king, but who had not yet been acknowledged by his people as the king.

When did this occur in the case of the Messiah? Immediately one who is familiar with the New Testament recalls the passage of Scripture which has come to be referred to as The Triumphal Entry in Matthew 21, Mark 11, Luke 19, and John 12, where the Messiah is presented as God's appointed King, but not accepted by His people as their Messiah, but rejected and ultimately crucified, "cut off" as Daniel 9:26 indicates. When was Messiah the Prince revealed? In April, AD 32, as recorded by history.[8]

Fourth, a question which is now answerable, having covered the previous three, what is a "week" as used in this passage? Clearly, the passage of time between the commandment of Artaxerxes and the time of the triumphal entry was more than sixty-nine weeks of seven days each. Clearly, the time which was designated as a week was a period of seven years for each week. This is not an unusual use of the term translated week, since it occurs in Genesis 29:27 in relation to Jacob's service for Rachel. This interpretation is confirmed, however, by the fact that 173,880 days transpired between the decree of Artaxerxes and the triumphal entry, as proven historically, and this is 69 (weeks) times 7 (years) times 360 (days in a biblical calendar year, see Revelation 11:3 and 12:6) which equals 173,880. Sir Robert Anderson, in his book *The Coming Prince*,[8] translates this very effectively into our modern calendar in the following way:

445 BC to AD 32 = 476 years = 476 x 365 = 173,740 days
(BC 1 to AD 1 is 2 years, not 3)
Add from March 14 to April 6 inclusive = 24 days
Add for leap years = 116 days
Total = 173,880 days

The time which has been spent in reaching this conclusion concerning the first sixty-nine weeks will be of great significance when we come to study the seventieth week and its details. The reader will be reminded to refer back to this question and its answer.

Fifth, what additional things will transpire? The city and the sanctuary will be destroyed, Daniel is told in Daniel 9:26. This was fulfilled in AD 70 by the Roman emperor Titus, even as to the description of the way in which it occurred, by a flood. But the narrative of the heavenly messenger goes on to describe the making of a firm covenant for "one week ... " and the breaking of that covenant by the stopping of the sacrifice and grain offering "in the middle of the week" (Dan. 9:27 NASB). There is also prophesied an "abomination of desolation" (Dan. 9:27). To what or whom does this refer? Our further study will seek to answer this question.

CHAPTER SIX

TEXT: MATTHEW 13:1–30

In the previous chapters we have seen how God revealed to and through the prophet Daniel the events leading up to the crucifixion of the Lord Jesus. Quite clearly, Daniel was also given additional truth, as we have already seen in part, regarding the future of his "people" and his "holy city" (Dan 9:24). But what additional facts are available regarding the time which the book of Daniel has revealed, and which is described as the "Times of the Gentiles"?

One of the key passages of the teaching of the Lord Jesus in relation to the job which has been given to us as believers during this period of the "Times of the Gentiles" is found in Matthew 13. It has truth that is applicable, as we shall see, to our time, as well as to the time when God will re-gather Israel.

In our opening chapter, we introduced the concept that the kingdom of heaven, which, as used generally in Matthew, referred to the earthly reign of Christ, the Messiah. The term "Kingdom of God" is used throughout Scripture to denote that realm in which all are found who are willingly subject to God, by faith, through His grace. It includes both Old and

New Testament believers, and is typified by the Hall of Fame of the faithful found in Hebrews 11. Though many struggle with the distinction between these two kingdoms, and many great theologians who were and are men of God have not recognized this distinction, the passage before us is one which makes the distinction very clear. Let us proceed to see the distinction.

The parable of the sower and the parable of the wheat and tares indicate six areas of contrast between the Kingdom of God and the kingdom of heaven.

The identity of the sower is the first area of contrast. In the parable of the sower, the interpretation (given by the Lord Himself, so it is accurate!) places no significance on the identification of the sower. He is referred to merely as "the sower," and there is no further identification given of this individual in the otherwise detailed interpretation which the Lord gives. On the other hand, in the parable of the wheat and tares, the sower is identified definitely as the Son of Man (v. 37), on the one hand, and the devil on the other hand (v. 39). The critical question is this–does the devil sow seed in the Kingdom of God? If one believes the answer is yes, there must be careful consideration of what the seed is.

Thus the second area of contrast is that of the seed. In the parable of the sower, the Lord Jesus explains to His disciples very carefully that "the seed is the Word of God" (Luke 8:11). Again, on the other hand, in the parable of the wheat and tares (seen only in the Gospel of Matthew) the good seed are described by the Lord Jesus as "the children of the kingdom," and the tares are "the children of the wicked one" (Matt. 13:38). It begins to grow clearer here that a distinction is being made by the Lord Jesus between the two parables. Obviously, the devil does not sow the seed of the Word of God, though he does, as explained by the Lord, sow those who are a part of his domain, the children of the wicked one.

The third area of contrast between these two parables of the kingdom concerns the conditions surrounding the act of sowing the seed. In the parable of the sower, the adverse conditions exist concurrent with the sowing. Some of the ground is described as good ground, but some is adversely hard; there are thorns which spring up to choke the plant; the birds come to carry away the seed; there are stones to prevent the seed from getting good root. In contrast, in the parable of the wheat and tares, the good seed is sown exclusively to the field. Later, and notice clearly that it is subsequent to the sowing of the good seed, the enemy sows the weeds. Again there is a clear contrast here, and those who are involved in "sowing the seed" of the Word of God in this day and age must recognize that "the heart is deceitful above all things, and desperately wicked" (Jer. 17:9) and this condition occurs prior to the sowing of the seed, not following.

The fourth area of contrast involves the way in which the crop is identified. In the parable of the sower, the identification is based on growth and fruit. That portion of the seed which survives in this first parable is described as bringing forth fruit, "some an hundredfold, some sixtyfold, some thirtyfold" (Matt. 13:8). However, in the parable of the wheat and tares, identification is too difficult to make until the time of harvest, and the farm laborers are specifically instructed not to attempt any action based on identification until the time of harvest.

The fifth area of contrast involves the distinctions in the methods used at the time of harvest. In the parable of the sower, the harvest is concerned only with the fruit produced. The thorns, the stones, the hard ground, have no significance in the process of the harvest, nor any apparent effect on the fruit which is harvested. In the parable of the wheat and tares, on the other hand, the tares are harvested first, and burned. Subsequent to that gathering and burning, the wheat is gathered into the barn.

The sixth and final contrast involves the harvester or harvesters. In the parable of the sower, the harvester is not identified. In clear contrast, in the parable of the wheat and tares, the harvesters are clearly identified by the Lord Jesus as the angels, sent forth at the "end of the age" by the Son of Man to first gather the tares to burn, and then the wheat into the barn. A critical question for the believer in the Lord Jesus Christ in this day and age to ask of himself is found here: Who will come to gather you? Do you look forward to the coming of an angel for you, or do you have your confidence in the passages which promise that the Lord Jesus will come personally for his saints? (John 14:3; 1 Thess. 4:16). Perhaps this does not seem to be of great significance, but remember, when studying interpretation, all the pieces must fit or the interpretation is not accurate.

It becomes apparent to even the almost casual observer that the Lord Jesus did not, as some would teach, merely enlarge upon the first parable of the sower with the parable of the wheat and the tares. Clearly, the Lord was describing two separate aspects of the Kingdom, one which is beyond the sphere and control of the adversary once the seed falls on good ground, the other in which the adversary has the opportunity to sow his children into the field.

The question to be asked is, what is the distinction and contrast? The one in the parable of the sower who received the seed into the good ground and brought forth fruit is, of necessity, one in whom the Holy Spirit has done a work to prepare his heart and who ministers to produce fruit through that new life, because of the seed of the Word of God being implanted in the heart. The Scripture makes it clear that fruit is produced through one's life only through the Holy Spirit, and not by means of self-effort (Gal. 5:22–23). By the same token, the wheat in the second parable must also be those who have had the same work done in their hearts. But these, in contrast to the first, are in a field where the children of the devil subsequently begin to appear and are so indistinguishable as to cause confusion as to the clear distinction between the two.

Notice the key distinction found in the first contrast. One group has the seed, the Word of God, sown in their hearts individually (note the explanation by the Lord which emphasizes the receiving of the Word), combined with understanding and reception, and bring forth fruit. The second are sown as children,

either children of the kingdom or children of the
wicked one.

The conclusion which one comes to in examining
this contrast is the same conclusion which is made in
the previous chapter in the distinction between the
Kingdom of God and the Kingdom of Heaven as
it is described in the Gospel of Matthew. Again, the
statement by *Vine* is clear:

*"With regard to the expressions 'the Kingdom of
God' and the 'Kingdom of the Heavens,' while they
are often used interchangeably, it does not follow
that in every case they mean exactly the same and
are quite identical."*[10]

It is in this passage that the similarities and
contrasts are shown, as the Lord teaches the distinction
between His eternal kingdom, the Kingdom of God,
of which all believers are a part, and His future earthly
kingdom, the kingdom of heaven, which is limited to a
specific time and an earthly sphere. This will be seen in
greater detail as the teachings of the Lord unfold in the
remainder of the parables in Matthew, particularly when
we come to the study of the Nature of the millennium
in the final chapter. As we look at the teachings of the
early chapters of Revelation and early prophecies of
Daniel, these details will also be confirmed.

CHAPTER SEVEN

TEXT: REVELATION 1–4

I t is here that we must return to the opening chapters of the book of Revelation in order to understand some of the prophetic distinctives of the church, the body and bride of Christ. Clearly, as we have seen in the teachings of our Lord in Matthew 13, there is a contrast between old covenant truth and new covenant truth. What is to be the course of events during this period of time in which we live, prior to the resumption of God's dealing with Israel as He has promised (Rom. 11:25)?

The early chapters of the book of Revelation address themselves to us as believers in this present day, as we are a part of the church. Why study the book of Revelation? Is it important to know the truth of this book? God's Word has something to say and to encourage us with as we approach what to many is a difficult and mysterious book. First, we need to remember that as the apostle Paul told Timothy in 2 Timothy 3:16, "**All** Scripture is given by inspiration of God and is **profitable** ... " (emphasis mine). Part of the way in which the study of Revelation can be profitable is indicated in 2 Peter 3:11, where the apostle Peter writing under the supervision of the Holy Spirit says, "Since all these things are to be destroyed in this way, what sort of people ought you to be in holy conduct and godliness ... " (NASB).

But perhaps most important of all is the verse that was mentioned early on in our study, Revelation 1:3, "Blessed is he who reads and those who hear the words of the prophecy, and heed the things which are written in it; for the time is near" (NASB). As difficult as the prophetic portions of the Word of God may be to understand, blessing is not promised to those who understand, but to the one who reads or hears, and the one who heeds! May it be the prayer and desire of each of our hearts to read and heed. As we are willing to do this, God the Holy Spirit will bring blessing as He has promised, and understanding as a result of His illuminating of the Word and guiding us "into all truth" (John 16:13).

There is one further reason for study in Revelation and in the prophetic portions of God's Word. In Revelation 1:6, we as believers in the Lord Jesus Christ are described as "a kingdom of priests." Priests are a group to whom truth is entrusted with the purpose of imparting that truth to others. Therefore, a responsibility is incumbent upon us to know the truth so that we can teach it, as Timothy was reminded in 2 Timothy 2:2, "And the things which you have heard from me in the presence of many witnesses, these entrust to faithful men, who will be able to teach others also" (NASB).

What is the Book of Revelation? It is the revelation of the person and work of Jesus Christ. Verse 1 is objective[11] (objective genitive)–not "from" but rather "of." Thus He is revealed in His glory in verses 13–18 of chapter 1. Note that the explanation of the symbols of the stars and the lampstands is in verse 20 and it is made clear that the stars are the messengers of the seven churches, and the lampstands are the seven churches.

It is given through the faithful servant, John, to write "what [he had] seen" (the Gospel of John), the things which are (chapters 2–4), and the things which shall be (chapters 5ff.). So we shall begin, as we have come to this place in both Daniel and Matthew, with the things which are, or what is happening now?

In chapter two of the book of Revelation, we are given, through the eyes of the apostle John, the message of the Lord Jesus Christ to the seven churches in Asia Minor, the area now in western Turkey. Each of these seven churches was an existing local church at the time, to which John had apparently had a ministry, and perhaps served as pastor amongst these churches.[12] Each of these churches, as has been pointed out by numerous Bible scholars throughout church history, apparently typifies the Church or the professing church at a particular time in history, prior to the coming of the Lord Jesus for His saints.[13] This is a customary use of prophecy, and one to which the Old Testament has introduced us, to see an immediate event, as well as to see the event typifying something yet future, as is seen, for instance, in Psalm 22 where David speaks of his experience but prophesies of the suffering Messiah. To each of these churches, as we shall see, the Lord reveals Himself in a special way, giving them, as it were, His personal evaluation of their ministry as to their strengths and weaknesses, and His statement as to the reward which will be theirs at His coming.

The first of the seven churches is the church in Ephesus. Christ speaks to them as the one in charge, the one who "holds the seven stars in His right hand, the One who walks among the seven golden lampstands." (Rev. 2:2). He speaks with this authority to this church in Ephesus, which typifies the church of the first century AD.[14]

In pointing out the strengths of the church at Ephesus, the great shepherd and pastor of the sheep mentions four things. He says that they are hardworking, "I know ... your toil" and their patience, "and perseverance" (Rev. 2:2). He commends them for the fact that they are discerning of falsehood in this same verse.

He does, however, point out that their critical weakness was a loss of the joy of service, they had "left their first love" (Rev. 2:3), and admonishes them to repent or He will remove their testimony. This admonition, as is typical of the great grace of God, is followed again by a commendation regarding their hatred of the Nicolaitans. This cult has had its influence throughout the history of the church. It was typified at this time by licentious behavior on the part of "laymen" and an expectation of proper behavior on the part of the "clergy." This is the beginning of a "hireling" concept which Jesus warned about in relation to shepherding in

John 10:12–13. There will be more said of this danger further on in this passage.

The church at Ephesus, which is admonished because of its lack of vitality and joy, is promised as its reward the tree of life, the eternal source of life. Again, God's graciousness towards His people is so great that one continues to marvel!

The second church to whom Christ speaks, is the church at Smyrna. This church typifies the church in the period from about AD 100–313.[15] Apparently the local church at Smyrna was undergoing persecution, as was the historical church which it typifies. Christ commends it for its works, its suffering, its poverty, and its strength under ridicule (Rev. 2:9), and He speaks to this church, not as the one in charge, but as the one who has suffered. Not only does He speak from this gracious perspective, but because of the persecution which this church is undergoing and the encouragement which is needed, there is no mention of any weakness. What great grace! The suffering one speaks comfort to His suffering church.

The fact that weaknesses are not mentioned also reminds us of the important truth expressed in 1 Peter 1:7, "That the proof of your faith, being more precious that gold which is perishable, even though tested by fire, may be found to result in praise and glory and honor at the revelation of Jesus Christ" (NASB). When we are tested, the impurities are removed by the fire, and this was true of Smyrna.

The reward promised to Smyrna was the crown of life, mentioned also in James 1:12 as a blessed reward for the one who "perseveres under trial." God's blessed, gracious care for His suffering church is clearly evident here.

The third church to receive Christ's message is Pergamum. He speaks to it as the Word of God, the two-edged sword, and commends them for their works and the fact that they "hold fast My name." (Rev. 2:13) and have not denied the faith. It is significant that this church typifies the church historically from about AD 313 to 590,[16] during the time of the question of Arianism–the denial of the deity of Christ. It was during this time that the Council of Trent affirmed the deity of Christ and encouraged the use of a doxology with every hymn in order to affirm the doctrine of the Trinity.

But there are some clear weaknesses pointed out in Pergamum. One was the doctrine of Balaam, which was the doctrine of a mixed multitude, lack of separation of God's people, where Balaam encouraged the intermarriage of Israel with the heathen. Historically, it is the period of time when the church, under the edict of Constantine enjoying political recognition, expands territorially without regard to the emphasis on personal faith in the Lord Jesus Christ as Savior. The church was losing its identity as God's family and becoming a religious or social institution rather than a spiritual body.

Its second weakness is the doctrine of the Nicolaitans. Apparently this was a problem in Pergamum. Where Ephesus is commended for their stand, Pergamum is warned about its compromise. Historically, the clergy had become separated from the people, and were even giving permission for the laity to sin, by the selling of "tolerances." What blasphemy to the concept of the kingdom of priests that we have been taught in Revelation 1.

The warning and the reward are knit closely together here. The "sword of My mouth" (v. 16) is promised by Christ if they do not repent. To the faithful, the hidden manna, the Word of God, is promised. We know that historically the written Word of God began to be available as it was canonized and copied and taught. How important is the verse, "the entrance of Thy words giveth light" (Ps. 119:130).

The fourth church to receive the message of the pastor is Thyatira. The message comes from the Pure One, the Glorious One, the Holy One, the One whose "eyes are like a flame of fire, and His feet are like burnished bronze" (Rev. 2:18). The strengths which the Lord records for Thyatira are its love, its faith, its perseverance, and the increase in its activity. It is significant that this church typifies the church during the Dark Ages from about AD 590 to 1500.[17] As this period drew to a close, activity was increasing with the opening signs of the Reformation.

The weaknesses of this church are significant, in that it typifies the historical position of the church which it represents so clearly. Jezebel is described as being tolerated by this church as a false teacher who calls herself a prophetess. The clear description is of a woman who has usurped authority, not called as a prophetess by God nor recognized with this gift by the local church, but usurping this authority by calling herself a prophetess (Rev. 2:20). How quickly 1 Timothy 2:12 comes to mind in this context, where Paul, under the guidance of the Holy Spirit says, "But I suffer not a woman to teach nor to **usurp** authority ... "(emphasis mine). This was the problem that so often has occurred in the history of the church, a false teacher who usurps authority, and how often has this false teaching been introduced by a woman!

It is significant that the reward for this church is clearly designed to meet its need. Christ promises authority from Himself and the clarity of enlightening truth as typified by the morning star.

The fifth church to whom Christ speaks is the church at Sardis. The message comes from the Chief Messenger and the Head of the Church. This church typifies the church from about AD 1500 to 1800.[18] Its strengths are described as having "a few people, even in Sardis" who are not defiled. Historically we see these as outstanding men of God, such as Luther, Calvin, Wycliffe, Hus, and many other great reformers, but from God's perspective they were certainly few.

Overall, the church was dead, Christ says in Revelation 3:1, and goes on to describe them as being asleep. To the few who are not tainted by this death, Christ promises as their reward the garments of eternal life; "They will walk with me in white, for they are worthy" (Rev. 3:4). How good God is to His family, those who believe by faith, no matter what their surroundings.

The sixth church to hear from its shepherd is the church in Philadelphia, and speaking is the Holy,

True, and All-Powerful One. Philadelphia typifies the believing church from 1800 to the rapture,[19] which has included such great men of God as Jonathan Edwards, D. L. Moody, Billy Sunday, Billy Graham, Charles Haddon Spurgeon, and many more. The Great Shepherd of the sheep describes this church as having a little strength, having kept His Word, and not denying His name. How different His evaluation from ours, as we look at our evangelization efforts and great missionary emphasis during these historical years, and yet Christ says we have "a little strength" (Rev. 3:8).

The weakness which is mentioned in regard to the Philadelphia church is the danger of being infiltrated by Satan and those of his synagogue and the fact that there is only a little power. But the Lord commends His church for their perseverance against the onslaught of the adversary, and promises that they will be kept from the time when Satan will have opportunity to test those that dwell on the earth. There will be more said of this later, but there are three key words in this promise; they are,

1 "KEEP you from ..." (v. 10), in Greek *it* is se *teresw ek* (*se teireiso ek*)[20] not *en(en.)* Literally, to keep you out from, not in. It is much the same as what is seen in the Old Testament in the distinction between Enoch's deliverance from judgment and Noah's. Enoch was taken out; Noah was delivered through. God's promise is that His church will be

taken out. As we have seen thus far in our discussions from the book of Matthew, there is a distinction between Israel and the Church.

2 "To TEST those" (v. 10). The word *peirazw* (*peiradzo*) is never used of a testing by God of the believer. It is used of the believer where the testing is to be self-imposed as in 2 Corinthians 12:5. It is used regularly of Satan tempting man to sin (Luke 4) but the Scripture teaches that God does not tempt the saints but protects them from undue temptation (1 Cor. 10:13; James 1:13).

3 "that DWELL upon the earth..."*katoikew* (*katoikeo*) is a strong word used to describe the fullness of the Godhead that dwells in Christ (Colossians 2:9), and of Christ indwelling the Christian (Eph. 3:17). It is not used of the believer as he dwells on earth but often of Israel and the nations. It is distinguished from *oikew* (*oikeo*) which is the normally used term for dwell and from *paroikew* (*paroikeo*) which the idea of sojourning. The believer is not described as a person who dwells (*katoikeo*) but who sojourns (*paroikeo*) (Phil. 3:20).[21]

The seventh church is the church of Laodicea. It is significant that the city of Laodicea was noted for its great commercial wealth and its Phrygian powder for the treatment of eye disorders. The message to Laodicea comes from the Creator and the fulfillment of all truth, to a church which has no strength and denies the truth.

Laodicea is described as the professing historical church and the church of the present day where Christ is outside seeking entrance, as a church which has no source of power. It is lukewarm and claims to be rich, needing nothing. Thus, this church has no strengths because the Head of the Church is not its head.

The message of Christ to this church is to buy His riches, to anoint their eyes with His balm, and to be clothed in His righteousness and not their own. This church is without reward, since Christ is still pictured as outside, seeking entrance. What a graphic portrait of the professing church today, yet without Christ.

"HE WHO OVERCOMES." Who is this that we are reminded of after each message to each church? First John 5:4 gives us the answer by saying, "[T]his is the victory that overcometh the world, even our faith," and Revelation 21:7 summarizes the reward of that faith when it says, "He who overcomes shall inherit these things, and I will be his God and he will be my son" (NASB). It is important to note that it is not perseverance, but faith in Christ that overcomes.

CHAPTER EIGHT

TEXT: MATTHEW 23:37–24:14

As we come to this central passage of Scripture, beginning here and ending at the conclusion of Matthew 25, we must recognize the fact that the entire discourse by our Lord is given in response to a question asked of Him by His disciples in Matthew 24:3.

It is also worthy of comment to note that the disciples asked the question immediately following some highly significant statements by the Lord Himself. In Matthew 23:37 He begins a lament over the city of Jerusalem, pronouncing that "your house is being left to you desolate" (NASB). Note that Luke 19:42–44 also, in parallel manner, contains this lament, and includes two significant statements: "If you had known in this day, even you, the things which make for peace! But now they have been hidden from your eyes" (Luke 19:42 NASB).

How significant that statement is when we compare it with the apostle Paul's statement in Romans 11:25 that "hardening has happened to Israel until the fullness of the Gentiles has come in" (NASB). It is also significant in relation to Paul's repetition of statements from the Old Testament regarding Israel's blindness in the same chapter of Romans.

The Lord Jesus not only comments in this way, but goes on to say that Jerusalem will be destroyed "because you did not recognize the time of your visitation" (Luke 19:44 NASB). How interesting it is that the term "visitation" in both Old and New Testament languages signifies the concept of looking over, an inspection, and that the father of John the Baptist spoke of this when he said, "Blessed be the Lord God of Israel; for he hath visited and redeemed his people" (Luke 1:68).

The prophets of the Old Testament, prophesying of the coming of the Messiah in judgment and glory, referred to that coming as a visitation. Zechariah said, "For the Lord of hosts hath visited his flock, the house of Judah and hath made them as his goodly horse in the battle" (Zech. 10:3). The prophet Zephaniah said, "For the Lord their God shall visit them and turn away their captivity" (Zeph. 2:7).

As a conclusion to the Lord's lament in Matthew 23, He makes this significant statement, "For I say to you, from now on you shall not see Me until you say, 'Blessed is He who comes in the name of the Lord'" (Matt. 23:39 NASB). Immediately following this statement, and the Lord's reiteration of the destruction of the temple in Matthew 24:2, the disciples ask Him, "When shall these things be?" What things? What had He just talked about? The destruction of Jerusalem and the temple and His coming as King! He had also just said that His coming as King would not be at that time, because Israel had not recognized Him as their King. So as He begins to answer these questions, we look first at the question in Matthew 24:3, and then, beginning at Matthew 24:4, the Lord's answer.

The question asked of the Lord by the disciples had three parts:

I   When shall these things be?

II   What shall be the sign of Thy coming?

III   What shall be the sign of the end of the age?

And the answer given by the Lord relates directly to those parts of the question. The answers are given by the Lord to answer the questions specifically.

In response to the question "WHEN shall these things be?" we have first reviewed the statement of Matthew 23:37–39 and Matthew 24:2 to see what things, and then must ask two additional questions to amplify our understanding of why the disciples asked the question.

What was the current hope of Israel? A nation under domination of a Gentile power was looking for the fulfillment of such prophecies as Micah 5:2, "But thou, Bethlehem Ephrathah, though thou be little among the thousands of Judah, yet out of thee shall he come forth unto me that is to be ruler in Israel, whose goings forth have been from of old, from everlasting."

They also looked for fulfillment of a prophecy like that of Isaiah 9:6–7,

"For unto us a child is born, unto us a son is given, and the government shall be upon his shoulder; and his name shall be called Wonderful, Counselor, The

Mighty God, The Everlasting Father, The Prince of Peace. Of the increase of his government and peace there shall be no end, upon the throne of David, and upon his kingdom, to order it, and to establish it with justice and with righteousness from henceforth even forever. The zeal of the Lord of hosts will perform this."

In addition, there is the fact that the disciples asking this question knew of the New Testament confirmation of these prophecies already heralded by the angels' announcement in Matthew 1:23, "Behold the virgin shall be with child, and shall bring forth a son, and they shall call his name Immanuel, which, being interpreted is, God with us." They also knew of the wise men's pronouncement in Matthew 2:2, "Where is he that is born King of the Jews? For we have seen his star in the east, and are come to worship him." Further, having seen and heard this testimony, the disciples had been convinced of the Messiahship of the Lord Jesus Christ themselves, as witnessed by the testimony of Nathaniel recorded in John 1:49, "Rabbi, thou art the Son of God; thou art the King of Israel."

What was the disciples' question after the death, burial, and resurrection of Christ? Acts 1:6 indicates that they were concerned if Christ would "at this time restore the kingdom to Israel." Restore, that is, from the domination of the Gentiles, whence it had been delivered at the times of the Assyrian and Babylon captivities. Remember that this is the concern of Daniel's heart when he is reading from the prophet Jeremiah, as recorded in Daniel 9, and he begins to pray that God's wrath will "turn away from Thy city Jerusalem, Thy holy mountain; for because of our sins and the iniquities of our fathers, Jerusalem and Thy people have become a reproach to all those around us" (Daniel 9:26 NASB). Remember, as well, that the answer to Daniel was that there would be a period of time during which Israel would continue to be dominated by the Gentiles.

What does Jesus give to His disciples as an answer to this same question? Jesus' answer in Matthew 24 includes several parts:

1 *Many antichrists will arise (v. 5).*
2 *There will be wars and rumors of wars (v. 6).*
3 *The end is not yet (v. 6).*
4 *Nation will rise against nation; famine, pestilence, and earthquakes will mark the "beginning of sorrows" (vv. 7–8).*

Here it is appropriate to ask a question that comes from our Gentile background, untaught as we are in the Old Testament Scriptures and not having the perspective of the Jew who had been taught regarding Israel's place in prophetic Scripture. What is the time of sorrows? To answer this we must refer to Jeremiah 30:1–9, with particular attention to verse 7. Notice that it is a time of which the prophet says, "Alas! for that day is great, There is none like it; And it is the time of Jacob's sorrow" (NASB). It is described by the prophet Jeremiah as a time of regathering of the nation Israel, a time of sorrow, a time of chastening and punishment in God's justice, a time of purifying, and a time of the raising up of their King.

Recall the parable of the leaven and what preceded the leaven. It was preceded by measures of meal that had been threshed, a time of purging by the Lord as prophesied by John the Baptist in Matthew 3:12, where he says, "And His winnowing fork is in His hand, and He will thoroughly clear His threshing floor; and He will gather His wheat into the barn, but He will burn up the chaff with unquenchable fire" (NASB). The Lord Jesus, as we shall see, points out this same truth, by mentioning a time of "great tribulation" in Matthew 24:21. We shall come to this later, but remember that the Jew, taught and instructed in the Old Testament, understood the phrase, the "beginning of sorrows" mentioned by the Lord in Matthew 24:8, to signify the beginning of birth pangs. Who or what will be born? The nation Israel will be born, under her Messiah, her promised King, with all the promised blessing which she has never yet achieved.

We return to Christ's narrative in answer to "When shall these things be?"

5 This gospel of the kingdom will be preached in all nations and then the end will come (v. 14). This is also a key answer.

First, notice carefully that it is the "gospel of the kingdom." What is the good news of the kingdom? (BE CAREFUL–we are talking here about the return of

Jesus Christ the Messiah at the time that Israel will say, "Blessed is He that cometh in the name of the Lord" (Matt. 23:39). This was the question that the disciples asked, "What shall be the sign of Thy coming?" and this is the answer the Lord is giving to that question.)

The good news of this kingdom to which the disciples are referring, (not the Kingdom of God, but the Messianic kingdom) is that it is "at hand"; therefore, it is time to repent. It is helpful here to remember to read Matthew 3:2–3, where the message is of the King and kingdom and contrast it with John 1 where the message is, "Behold the Lamb," a message of salvation for all, and also with Matthew 21:9 where the message is "Hosanna! Blessed is He that cometh in the name of the Lord!"

But it is also important to note, as pointed out by *Vine*, that the word repent in the New Testament always, except in Luke 17:3–4, signifies repentance from sin.[22] For this reason, it is clear that those who enter the kingdom of heaven are believers in the Lord Jesus as Messiah and Savior ("...they shall look on Him whom they have pierced." John 19:37). In explaining the gospel of the Kingdom, Joseph Good writes:

"This ... was called the 'basar,' which means 'good news,' and is commonly known as the 'gospel.' Hundreds of years before the Messiah's birth in Bethlehem, the 'basar' was well known and well defined; every Jewish child was reared on these precepts. The 'basar' was not the Messiah, rather the Messiah was the agent of the 'basar.' This

'good news' contained the following: the universal reign of G–d, the re–establishment of the House of David, the future glory of an Israel returned to G–d, the ingathering of the exiles, the resurrection of the dead, and the reward and punishment in the last judgment. "[23]

Who will preach this gospel? The Lord Jesus does not tell us here, but when we turn to the book of Revelation we see a remnant of the Jews, 144,000 of them in Revelation 7:3–8 and two witnesses in Revelation 11:3–12. To these are committed responsibility of being God's witness and testimony during this period of trouble. This concept is emphasized in Revelation 12:17, which tells of the, "Remnant ... which have the testimony of Jesus" (the name meaning Savior) "Christ" (the name meaning King – Messiah).

Again, it should be noted that of those who hear the message and observe the testimony of the 144,000 and of the two witnesses and repent, many are martyred for their faith and are clothed in white robes and stand before the throne of the Lamb in heaven (See Rev. 7:9–16). As throughout all ages, faith results in becoming a part of God's family (Heb. 11:1–6). But it also seems clear that the ministry of the 144,000 and the witnesses will not be to those who have already heard the gospel and rejected it, because they are mentioned in 2 Thessalonians 2:11–12: "God will send upon them a deluding influence so that they might believe what is false, in order that they all may be judged who did not believe the truth, but took pleasure in wickedness"

(NASB). Notice that they "did not believe" at some prior opportunity, probably while the church was preaching the gospel of God's grace. But notice that God's grace continues to extend to those who have not heard the message, so that "every mouth may be stopped, and all the world become guilty before God" (Rom. 3:19). But what else will occur before the end comes?

The Lord Jesus, in responding to the question of the disciples as to the sign of His coming, refers to the "abomination of desolation spoken of by Daniel the prophet" (Matt. 24:15) and proceeds to say that upon seeing this abomination the listeners can expect that there will be great tribulation.

The importance of this statement should not be overlooked in relation to the chronology of events. This explanation by our Lord is in answer to the question, "What shall be the sign of Thy coming?" (Matt. 24:3). These are the signs prior to His coming. This time of sorrow and great tribulation will take place prior to His coming. What does God's Word say about this time. We have already looked at some of the prophecies in Jeremiah regarding this time. We shall see more about this period of time as we look at Revelation to make comparison.

CHAPTER NINE

TEXT: REVELATION 6–8

It is important as we come to the time known as the tribulation, the "time of Jacob's trouble" (Jer. 30:7), that we also understand the term the "Day of the Lord"–a term used repeatedly in the Old Testament, particularly by the prophets. It designates a period of time in which God, as prophesied, intervenes directly in the affairs of men. It begins with the time of judgment that is introduced in Revelation beginning with chapter 6, and ends following Christ's earthly kingdom with the "Day of God," which is the prophetic designation of the end of this present heaven and earth (2 Pet. 3:12).

The prophecy of Joel speaks directly to the time known as the Day of the Lord and is very descriptive of the judgments that will take place during that time. It is clearly a time that begins with judgment, as Joel 2:1 indicates, when the prophet Joel is led to write, "Blow the trumpet in Zion, and sound an alarm in my holy mountain. Let all the inhabitants of the land tremble; for the day of the Lord cometh, for it is near at hand."

Certainly this is the same joyous occasion to which the believer in the Lord Jesus Christ is encouraged by the apostle Paul to be looking to and to be comforted by, when with "the voice of the archangel and the trumpet of God ... the dead in Christ will rise first. Then we who are alive and remain shall be caught up together with them in the clouds to meet the Lord in the air" (1 Thess. 4:16–17 NASB. See *The Last Trumpet* by this author available on Kindle).

Regarding the Jewish understanding of the term "Day of the Lord," Good says:

"The Day of the L–rd is complex in its makeup, because several different programs of G–d are going on at the same time. On the first day of the period knows as the Day of the L–rd, the Shofar will sound; the resurrection of the righteous...will occur.... On earth, those who are not caught away will be thrown into the 'time of trouble,' most commonly known as the 'birthpangs of the Messiah,' but also called the 'wrath of G–d,' 'tribulation' and 'indignation.' During this time the earth will be purged from sin."[24]

As we look at this period of time we shall see more of the Nature, the Source, and the purpose of the tribulation.

Beginning in Revelation 6, we are given the information regarding each of the seven seals that are on the book which the Lamb has been declared worthy to open (Rev. 5:5).

A seven-sealed document was a last testament of an individual, and required all surviving testators of the seven who had witnessed the last will and testament to be present in order for the document to be opened. Thus the phrase "no man worthy to open the seals" has to do with the witness(es) to the testament. But because the Lamb is risen from the dead, and therefore a surviving testator, He is the one worthy to open the seals of His testament, His new covenant or testament with Israel as promised in Jeremiah 31:31, where the prophet says, " 'Behold, days are coming,' declares the Lord, 'when I will make a new covenant with the house of Israel and with the house of Judah' " (NASB).

The NATURE OF THE TRIBULATION is described for us in the first six seals. The four horsemen of the apocalypse are the first four seals, and are well known as symbols of disaster, even amongst those who have little biblical knowledge. It is interesting to observe, however, that most who do not read the book of Revelation carefully do not properly interpret the first horseman, the first seal.

The first seal is the first horseman, the symbol of worldwide government, as indicated by the fact that he is given a crown and a bow, as symbols of his authority to go forth "conquering and to conquer" (Rev. 6:2). Would that those in the world today, many of them Christians who are untaught, would understand the significance and danger of the movement toward one world–a worldwide government. This worldwide government is the first indication of the tribulation. As we remember the words of the Lord Jesus to His disciples in Matthew, we remember that He indicated that "many will come in My name" (Matt. 24:5), and certainly the culmination of this will be the revelation of the Antichrist. In order for him to be successful, the judgment of worldwide government must take place.

The second seal, the second horseman, is war. The judgment of war is clearly stated, as the horseman has the power to "take peace from the earth" (Rev. 6:4). Thus, the symbolism is very clear. Again, the human solution to the world's problems is world government which would, in man's judgment, insure worldwide peace. But notice that as worldwide government comes, peace is taken from the earth.

The third seal, the third horseman, is the judgment of famine and economic disaster, made clear by the description. Consider this: If the world of our time is nearing the "last days," as all signs would indicate, what single factor would override all nationalistic influences and allow a one-world government to be instituted? Only one thing, as we see the world around us today with its varied political institutions, and that one thing is economic disaster. The individual who claimed to have the answer to the world economic crisis that will develop will be the one who would easily be recognized as a world messiah—the Antichrist.

As an integral part of the first three horseman, the fourth seal, the fourth horseman, is death. This judgment causes the death of twenty-five percent of the world's population by strife, by famine, by pestilence, and by the attack of wild beasts; in effect a loss of man's dominion over the animal kingdom because of man's disobedience to God's Word. Our present perspective, with modern medicine and technology, makes it impossible for us to perceive of so huge a loss of human life, but God's Word promises this judgment, and His Word is sure. As we consider this awful judgment, how great is our task to make the gospel of God's grace known, before God's judgment begins.

Having completed the look at the four horseman in the first four seals of judgment, we come to the fifth seal. This is the seal of martyrdom, and we have the description of those who are "slain because of the word of God, and because of the testimony which they had maintained" (Rev. 6:10 NASB). These are, no doubt, the same as those who are seen around the throne of God in Revelation 7:9ff, who are described in Revelation 7:14 as those "who have come out of great tribulation and have washed their robes, and made them white in the blood of the Lamb." Why have they "come out"? Because of the requirement of the world ruler, the Antichrist, that in order to buy or sell one must receive the "mark of the beast" in their forehead or right hand (Rev. 13:16–17). Thus, in order to buy food, one must worship the beast. These who are believers in Christ have thus come out of this tribulation through death for refusing this mark.

The sixth seal is the seal of natural disasters. The term natural is used advisedly, not to denote that they occur without source, but these are truly "acts of God" in which He uses natural phenomenon to bring judgment upon men and nations. Earthquakes, darkening of the sun, and unusual activities in the solar system, as well as upheaval in the Earth's structure are indicated so that men are brought to the realization that this is the "great day of His wrath" (Rev. 6:17). It is of great significance to note that those whose eschatological interpretation leads them to attribute the descriptions of the book of Revelation to the time of the fall of Jerusalem would be under no such delusion were they to be present at this time.

Those who are described as undergoing this judgment have a clear indication of the SOURCE OF THE TRIBULATION, that it is God Himself. It would be appropriate to look further in prophetic Scripture to verify the accuracy of this perspective in order to determine if these who are described as saying to the rocks and the mountains to fall upon them are accurate in believing that the source of this great trouble is God, the Judge.

First, notice that in Revelation 6:16–17 they describe it as the "wrath of the Lamb." To whom has all judgment been committed? To the second person of the Trinity, the Lord Jesus Christ. We are told in John 5:22, "For the Father judgeth no man, but hath committed all judgment unto the Son," and we are also told in John 9:39 that Jesus said, "For judgment I am come into this world...." In Jeremiah 30:1–11, the prophet Jeremiah is directed to tell the nation Israel that God will sit in judgment against His people Israel. The time is described in Jeremiah 30:7 as "the time of Jacob's trouble, but he shall be saved out of it." God promises, through Jeremiah, that He will not, however, make a full end of Israel, but "will correct thee in measure, and will not leave thee altogether unpunished" (Jer. 30:11).

The prophet Amos speaks extensively of this period of time as the time of God's judgment against

Israel for their refusal to heed His prophets. He reminds them that the coming of the Messiah will be preceded by a time of judgment, when he says, "Woe unto you that desire the day of the Lord! To what end is it for you? The day of the Lord is darkness, and not light" (Amos 5:18). He further says that the Lord "will sift the house of Israel among all nations, as grain is sifted in a sieve ... all the sinners of the people shall die by the sword... In that day I will raise up the tabernacle of David that is fallen" (Amos 9:10–11).

Following judgment, Israel will receive their Messiah, but the sifting will come first, and it will come from the Lord, as promised by Moses in his parting address to Israel in Deuteronomy 4:30, "When thou art in **tribulation**, and all these things are come upon thee, **even in the latter days**, if thou turn to the Lord thy God ... He will not forsake thee" (emphasis mine). Note that Moses prophesied of tribulation for Israel in the latter days, the time of the end, and that he did not say, "If thou art in tribulation," but "**When...**". The "end of the age" was what the disciples asked about, and this is what Moses had prophesied to occur in the latter days. So, clearly, as far as Israel is concerned, the source of the tribulation is the Lord Jesus, dealing with judgment upon His disobedient nation, Israel.

Thus the source of the tribulation is the Judge of all the Earth. But what is the PURPOSE OF THE TRIBULATION? Clearly, with the prophecies we have already seen in considering the source of the Tribulation, one of the key purposes of the Tribulation is to prepare

Israel for the millennial kingdom of Christ. Ezekiel 20:33–40 deals with this in terms which cannot easily be mistaken when the prophet Ezekiel is led to write,

" 'As I live,' declares the Lord God, ' surely with a mighty hand and with an outstretched arm and with wrath poured out, I shall be king over you...and I shall bring you into the wilderness of the peoples, and there I shall enter into judgment with you face to face...And I shall make you pass under the rod...'" (Ezekiel 20:33, 35, 37, NASB).

The prophet Zechariah also is led by the Holy Spirit to speak of this as the purpose of this time, when he says in Zechariah 13:9,

"And I will bring the third part through the fire, Refine them as silver is refined, And test them as gold is tested, They will call on My name, And I will answer them; I will say, 'They are my people,' And they will say, 'The Lord is my God' " (NASB).

And so it is clear that the focus of this time which the prophets have described as the time of Jacob's trouble is, at least in part, directed specifically toward the people of Israel. But there is an additional purpose as well, which is taught in Scripture.

Both the prophets Isaiah and Jeremiah point out the fact that the purpose of the tribulation is to judge unbelieving men and nations. "Behold, evil is going forth from nation to nation...And those slain by the Lord on that day shall be from one end of the earth to the other" (Jer. 25:32–33), are the words of the prophet Jeremiah as he describes this time of judgment. The prophet Isaiah says, "For behold the Lord is about to come out from His place to punish the inhabitants of the earth for their iniquity." (Isa. 26:21).

This teaching of the Old Testament from the prophets to Israel is reinforced by the apostle Paul in the New Testament teaching to the Thessalonian church, when he writes, "in order that they all may be judged who did not believe the truth, but took pleasure in wickedness" (2 Thess. 2:12). It is important that Paul, in giving this teaching regarding judgment, does it in connection with his teaching regarding the revelation of the "lawless one ... whose coming is in accord with the activity of Satan, with all power and signs and false wonders" (2 Thess. 2:9 NASB).

Given the indication of the awful judgment to come upon Israel and the inhabitants of the earth during this time, is there any hope for anyone to survive this period of God's wrath? Only through God's infinite grace, which is ever operable. Who will those be who are preserved, miraculously, during this time of judgment?

First, the Word of God speaks of a group of people known as "the elect." Who are they? Revelation 7:4–8 describes them clearly. They are a group of the nation Israel, twelve thousand from each tribe, one hundred and forty–four thousand in all. Since the Holy Spirit guides the apostle John to go into detail in delineating each tribe and the specific number from each tribe, it is clear that His desire is to make clear that these are from the nation Israel.

None of us who are part of the household of faith, who have become Abraham's seed through that faith, can lay claim to being from a particular tribe of Israel if we are Gentiles! It is clear that God intends to convey that this group of people is a righteous remnant of Israel, as is found in the Old Testament and described as the "remnant" or the "elect" in those passages. Perhaps the key passage in the Old Testament is found in Ezekiel 9:4, "And the Lord said to him, 'Go through the midst of the city, even through the midst of Jerusalem and put a mark on the foreheads of the men who sigh and groan over all the abominations which are being committed in its midst.' "

When this passage is compared with the passage before us in Revelation 7:3, where the angel says to the four angels who are given power to harm the earth, "Do not harm the earth or the sea or the trees, until we have sealed the bond–servants of our God on their foreheads," there is certainly a striking parallel. This is made most clear from the prophecy of Joel 2:32, where Joel says:

"The sun will be turned into darkness, And the moon into blood, Before the great and awesome day of the Lord comes. And it will come about that whoever calls on the name of the Lord Will be delivered; For on Mount Zion and in Jerusalem There will be those who escape, As the Lord has said, Even among the survivors whom the Lord calls" (NASB).

In addition, these are also mentioned by the prophet Daniel, in Daniel 12:1, where speaking of this time of tribulation, he says, "And there will be a time of distress such as has never occurred since there was a nation until that time; and at that time your people, everyone who is found written in the book, will be rescued" (NASB). Again, it is very clear that these are Daniel's people, people of his nation, Israel.

Note carefully that those who escape the judgment are the called ones, literally the elect ones. But it is important that these are delivered in a particular way. How does this take place?

First, as we have seen, they receive the "seal of God in their foreheads" (Rev. 7:3; 14:1). Second, there is miraculous intervention to prevent their destruction by Satan, as seen in Revelation 12:1–6 and 13–17, which describes the way in which this remnant of the nation Israel is preserved in a place "prepared by God" for her preservation. Third, and most importantly, these elect are preserved not because of personal merit, not because of personal effort, but by God's matchless grace through personal faith.

Revelation 12:11 describes it in this way, "And they overcame him because of the blood of the Lamb and because of the word of their testimony...." How great is God's grace, that even during the time of His fierce judgment, he delivers those who believe in the work of the Lord Jesus Christ! But God's love for His people is manifested in yet another way, because the Lord Jesus, in describing the awfulness of this period of judgment, says that "for the sake of the elect those days shall be cut short" (Matt. 24:22 NASB).

What is the job that the elect, this group of 144,000, are given during this time? Revelation 12:17

indicates that it is their responsibility to "keep the commandments of God and hold to the testimony of Jesus." In addition, Micah 5:7 indicates that the "remnant of Jacob will be among many peoples like dew from the Lord, like showers on vegetation..." (NASB). The refreshing news of the gospel is to come from the mouths of these of God's remnant.

With this in mind, it is important to note that the Great Commission will be completely fulfilled by this remnant, as prophesied by the Lord Himself in Matthew 24:14, where in answer to the question asked by the disciples as to when the end of the age would come, He said, "And this gospel of the kingdom shall be preached in the whole world for a witness to all the nations, and then the end shall come" (NASB). Note that this is after the indication by the Lord that a time of tribulation has begun, and when we couple this information with the disciples question it becomes clear what "end" is being discussed.

Note also that it is a specific gospel, the good news of the kingdom, not the news that John gave when he said, "Behold, the Lamb of God who takes away the sin of the world" (John 1:29 NASB). It is closely related to the gospel, which is referred to in Zechariah 8:23, "In those days ten men from all the nations will grasp the garment of a Jew saying, 'Let us go with you, for we have heard that God is with you.' " (NASB) A message uniquely suited to a Jew, a message which comes uniquely through a Jewish remnant, a message which causes those who hear it to be drawn to Jews because of the knowledge that God is with them, what message is that? The message, of course, is, "The kingdom of heaven is at hand" (Matt. 10:7 NASB).

Who will hear and what will be the response to this message? There will be those who hear this message from the 144,000 who respond by faith and believe in the Lord Jesus Christ, the Messiah. They are the ones described in Revelation 7:14, "who come out of the great tribulation, and they have washed their robes and made them white in the blood of the Lamb" (NASB). This great multitude, standing before the throne of God and before the Lamb, described in the seventh chapter of Revelation as being clothed in white robes with palms in their hands, are those who have been martyred because of their faith. Why have they been martyred? Because, quite simply, as those who have placed their faith in Christ they are no longer able to worship the beast or receive his mark in their foreheads, and therefore are no longer permitted to buy and sell food. They may be killed for their faith, or they may simply starve to death, but they are with the Lord because of their faith. This concept is borne out by the passage in Revelation 6:9–11, describing the fifth seal as one of martyrdom of believers, those who are killed because of their faith and who await "their brethren who were to be killed even as they had been … " (Rev. 6:11 NASB).

Additionally, regarding these who are saved during the time of the tribulation, the witness given to them comes from the 144,000, as we have seen. The gospel also comes to them from the two witnesses, the account of whom is found in Revelation 11:1–14. These who are saved are not those who have heard prior to the tribulation. The apostle Paul, writing to the Thessalonians in 2 Thessalonians 2:1–12 makes this very clear. He summarizes all that he says in verse 11, "For this cause God shall send them strong delusion, that they should believe a lie, in order that they all might be judged .... "

The Scripture makes it very clear that those who have heard the gospel prior to this time of tribulation will not have a second chance as a result of the ministry of the 144,000 or the two witnesses. Quite clearly, their ministry is to the unreached of the world, those who have never heard the Gospel, and as a result of their ministry, countless souls will believe.

As we return to the narrative of Revelation chapter 8 regarding the events of the tribulation, we return to the sequence of the opening of the seven seals. The seventh seal is opened and reveals events so awesome that there is "silence in heaven for about half an hour" (Rev. 8:1 NASB). The opening of the seventh seal reveals seven angels who are given seven trumpets to sound. Trumpets are significant to the nation Israel because of the instruction given to Israel as recorded in Numbers 10. Trumpets were to be used to notify the nation of events of significance, when they were to assemble, when their leaders were to assemble, when they were to march, and when there was an "alarm" signifying danger or attack. This last item is particularly significant in view of the statement of Joel 2:1, where the prophet says, "Blow a trumpet in Zion, And sound an alarm on My holy mountain! Let all the inhabitants of the land tremble, for the day of the Lord is coming; Surely it is near" (Joel 2:1 NASB).

Thus, there are seven alarms sounded as to the judgment to be poured out, each of them is specific as to the judgment to be poured out. There is no need for extended comment on each of these judgments, and since they are specifically described we shall comment regarding their total effect in summary.

The first trumpet is sounded and a judgment follows of hail and fire in which one-third of all vegetation on the Earth is destroyed and all green grass. The second trumpet is sounded and a judgment like a "mountain burning with fire" causes the destruction of one-third of all sea life and one-third of all ships. The third trumpet is sounded and a star of wormwood causes one-third of all fresh waters to be made poisonous, which in turn causes the death of many.

The fourth trumpet sounds and the sun, moon, and stars are smitten, causing natural light to be diminished by one-third. It is particularly significant here that this causes the lights to be obscured for one-third of the time of day and of night, rather than one-third reduction in light intensity, which might be attributed to manmade causes. The fifth trumpet sounds and a star from heaven is given a key to the bottomless pit to release locusts to torment men. No doubt this "star" from heaven is the one referred to in Isaiah 14:12 as the "star of the morning" (NASB). As the leader of the rebellious host, Lucifer releases, under permission from the Judge of all the Earth, legions of his demons to torment men. This is borne out by the description of the locusts in Revelation 9:1–11, particularly when the fact that they are described as having "a king over them, the angel of the abyss; his name in Hebrew is Abaddon, and the Greek he has the name Apollyon" (Rev. 9:11 NASB). The sixth trumpet sounds and four angels are given the authority to kill one-third of mankind, but even still, in spite of these awesome judgments, mankind does not repent, verses 20 and 21 of Revelation 9 tell us.

The seventh trumpet sounds, as recorded in Revelation 11:15. This signifies the culmination of the time of judgment and the establishing of the Kingdom of Christ. As in any descriptive narrative, there is a chain of narrative that must backtrack at times. John's narrative has described the "wrath of the Lamb" or God's judgments on Earth to be carried out throughout the tribulation. There are some additional details which need to be covered, some of which have been alluded to already, and which John will cover in greater detail. In addition, he will backtrack, so to speak, and will describe additional events of this period of time and some additional final acts of God which will take place before the seventh trumpet is actually sounded. For this reason, there appears to be some confusion in the narrative, because the kingdom is proclaimed, and then nothing appears to happen. Take the time to see the big picture and make the pieces fit together—we will proceed to do that.

But first, let us summarize the judgments we have seen thus far—that is, the judgments included in the seven seals, which, of course, include the seven trumpets. Within these judgments, great phenomena occur which result in death and destruction. Within the first six seals, the complete delineation of the amount of death and destruction is not made clear, but when we come to the seventh seal, there is a tabulation of the destruction of one-third of the earth's vegetation, one-third of sea life and shipping, and one-third of the world's population in addition to those killed in conjunction with the other judgments and the one-fourth of the population apparently killed by the judgment of the fourth seal, that is the fourth horseman, Death.

As we consider the tremendous loss of life occurring in these judgments, and recognize that this is not the end of the judgments, one must certainly come to an understanding of the words of the Lord Jesus, when he said as recorded in Matthew 24:21, "For then shall be great tribulation, such as has not occurred since the beginning of the world until now, nor ever shall" (NASB).

CHAPTER TEN

TEXT: REVELATION 10–16

We come now to the narrative of the prophecy of John regarding the events leading up to the Battle of Armageddon and the end of the tribulation. This first portion of this passage could be titled, "The Prominent Personages of the Tribulation," since it deals with the individuals and nations involved. The passage begins with the prophecy of the seven thunders. Nothing is told us of this prophecy. John is directed to seal up the prophecy, and the declaration is then made that there is to be no further delay.

We are then immediately introduced to the first of the prominent personages, the two witnesses. There are three questions that should be answered in relation to these individuals. The first question is, Who are they?

These witnesses are not clearly identified by name, but their power is clearly like that of Moses and Elijah. Some credence to this identification is given in view of their presence on the Mount of Transfiguration (Matt. 17:3), but even more so by the prophecy of Malachi 4:5, "Behold, I am going to send you Elijah the prophet before the coming of the great and terrible day of the Lord" (NASB).

Certainly this is emphasized in the words of the Lord as He makes a distinction between John the Baptist and Elijah in Matthew 17:11–12, when asked if Elijah must come before the King comes, He says, "Elijah is coming and will restore all things; but I say to you, that Elijah already came, and they did not recognize him, but did to him whatever they wished" (NASB). The Lord Jesus does not say that Elijah will not come, but that John the Baptist fulfilled Elijah's ministry at the first advent, and that Elijah will personally come prior to the second advent. No further details are given as to the identity of these witnesses except as to their power, which is described in Revelation 11:6 as follows: "These have the power to shut up the sky, in order that rain may not fall during the days of their prophesying; and they have power over the waters to turn them into blood, and to smite the earth with every plague, as often as they desire" (NASB). Certainly this description of the power of the two witnesses corresponds very closely to the power given to Elijah and to Moses in the Old Testament.

The second question about these witnesses is, When do they testify? They are called upon to minister during the last half (forty-two months) of the tribulation; specifically, during the time when the remnant—the 144,000 who are sealed to pass through the tribulation and to be witnesses of the kingdom—are hidden in the wilderness and cannot continue their active witness. (This protection is delineated in Revelation 12:6, 14–17, where the remnant is pictured as the woman who gave birth to the male child who is to rule all the Earth. As a result of the attack of the dragon, she is protected by God in the wilderness for one thousand two hundred and sixty days, or forty-two months, or three and one-half years; the last half of the tribulation).

The third question flows logically from the second, What do the two witnesses do? Their responsibility is to prophesy during the latter half of the tribulation (Rev. 11:3). They are miraculously protected from harm by the power given them, "And if anyone desires to harm them, fire proceeds out of their mouth and devours their enemies ... "(Rev. 11:5 NASB). Because the Antichrist has broken his covenant with Israel, the remnant of Israel can no longer move about freely and is confined in the wilderness. But God is never without a witness, even when things appear beyond hope. He is sovereign, and these two witnesses have the responsibility to make the good news known even in these impossible times.

As the narrative continues in Revelation, we are introduced to additional prominent personages. As we have already noted, the nation Israel is described in chapter 12:1–2 and again in verses 5 and 6. The virgin birth of our Lord Jesus Christ is alluded to when the woman is described as being in labor, and the birth of the male child who is to rule all nations with a rod of iron who then is caught up to the throne of God, is certainly a clear reference to the Lord Jesus.

Next in the narrative, in verses 3 and 4 of Revelation 12, Satan and his historic rebellion against God is seen. His influence over one-third of the angels in heaven is described, as well as his historic attempts to destroy Christ at His birth, as evidenced by the edict of Herod to destroy all children under two years of age recorded in Matthew 2:16–18. (Certainly this was not the only such attempt on the Davidic line and Satan's attempt to defeat God's plan of redemption, but it is the one apparently described in this passage).

Then, as already indicated, Christ is caught up to heaven. Immediately following that description is the description of the believing remnant protected during the tribulation. Why the great compression of time here? God is dealing in this period with His nation, Israel. Since God set Israel aside following her rejection of her Messiah, Israel's history left off at Christ's ascension, and resumes with God once again dealing with her during the tribulation. It seems strange to us, from the perspective of God's dealing with the Gentiles and the establishing of the bride of Christ, the Church, to view this great chasm in prophetic time, but remember that this has always been the case. God's revelation regarding Israel, His dealing with His earthly, temporal people, has been thoroughly prophesied and documented. God's dealing with His heavenly, eternal people, the Church of Jesus Christ, is a "mystery which for ages has been hidden in God ... " (Eph. 3:9 NASB). Thus, it is not unusual, nor unexpected that the narrative regarding God's dealing with Israel should ignore other time periods. In commenting on this, Sir Robert Anderson says:

> *"According to the book of Kings, Solomon began to build the temple in the 480th year after the children of Israel were come out of the land of Egypt*

[I Kings 6:1]. This statement, than which none could, seemingly, be more exact, has sorely puzzled chronologers. By some it has been condemned as a forgery, by others it has been dismissed as a blunder; but all have agreed in rejecting it. Moreover, Scripture itself appears to clash with it. In his sermon at Psidian Antioch St. Paul epitomizes thus the chronology of this period of the history of his nation: forty years in the wilderness; 450 years under the Judges, and forty years of the reign of Saul; making a total of 530 years. To which must be added the forty years of David's reign and the first three years of Solomon's; making 573 years for the very period which is described in Kings as 480 years. Can these conclusions, apparently so inconsistent, be reconciled?

If we follow the history of Israel as detailed in the book of Judges, we shall find that for five several periods their national existence as Jehovah's people was in abeyance. In punishment for their idolatry, God gave them up again and again, and 'sold them into the hands of their enemies.' They became slaves to the king of Mesopotamia for eight years, to the king of Moab for eighteen years, to the king of Canaan for twenty years, to the Midianites for seven years, and finally to the Philistines for forty years. But the sum of 8 + 18 + 20 + 7 + 40 years is 93 years, and if 93 years be deducted from 573 years, the result is 480 years. It is obvious, therefore, that the 480 years of the book of Kings from the Exodus to the temple is a mystic era formed by eliminating

*every period during which the people were cast off
by God. If, then, this principle were intelligible to
the Jew in regard to history, it was both natural and
legitimate to introduce it in respect of an essentially
mystic era like that of the seventy weeks.*"[25]

During this time period, another prominent
personage is presented: Michael the archangel, the one
who is described as "your prince" (Dan. 10:21 NASB)
when speaking to Daniel, a prophet of Israel. War in
heaven takes place in Revelation 12:7–12, and Michael
and his angels defeat Satan and his angels and Satan is
cast out of heaven. Angry at his defeat, Satan attempts
to destroy the remnant of Israel, who is miraculously
delivered by God's intervention on their behalf, so that
the earth opens and swallows up the flood caused by
Satan.

The introduction to the prominent personage
of the Antichrist, described as the beast in Revelation
13:2, and the political system he commands, typified
by the ten horns or kingdoms, and the false prophet,
described as a second beast in Revelation 13:11, is
one of the pivotal passages of the description of the
tribulation. There are several key things that must be
noted in conjunction with these personages. First, the
political system which the Antichrist commands, the
ten kingdoms and the false prophet are in league with
the harlot of Babylon until the end of the tribulation,
just prior to the Battle of Armageddon (see Rev. 17:7).

This marriage of a world community political
system and an ecumenical world church will be Satan's
counterfeit attempt to provide peace and unity for the

world. It will be, in all reality, an attempt to counterfeit the kingdom of heaven, which Christ will set up after the Battle of Armageddon. Second, the power of this beast, the Antichrist, comes from Satan, the dragon, in order that men might worship Satan, "and they worshiped the dragon, because he gave his authority to the beast ... " (Rev. 13:4 NASB).

Third, there is a clever attempt to counterfeit the death and resurrection of Christ, so that men might be deceived as indicated in Revelation 13:3, "And I saw one of his heads as if it had been slain, and his fatal wound was healed. And the whole earth was amazed and followed after the beast" (NASB). Clearly, signs and wonders are not alone a proof of truth. Fourth, the entire world will follow and worship the beast, except those who are believers in the Lord Jesus Christ as John tells us in Revelation 13:8, where he says, "And all who dwell on the earth will worship him, everyone whose name has not been written from the foundation of the world in the book of life of the Lamb who has been slain" (NASB).

Fifth, quite clearly, this individual is the one prophesied of in Daniel 9:26–27 as the "prince that shall come" who will "make a firm covenant with the many for one week, but in the middle of the week he will put a stop to sacrifice and grain offering, and on the wing of abominations will come one who makes desolate" (NASB).

Clearly, this is also the one who is referred to by the Lord Himself as the "ABOMINATION OF DESOLATION which was spoken of through Daniel the prophet ... " (Matt. 24:15 NASB). The reason this correlation can be made is because of the time frame made clear by the Lord that when that covenant is broken there will be a great tribulation, that is, even more intense than that which had been preceding, and that the flight of the Jewish people would occur in conjunction with that time. What flight? The flight to avoid the attack of the dragon, Satan himself, already described in Revelation 12.

In addition, the strong correlation between the description of the Beast and his actions in Revelation 13 and the beast, his ten horns, and his actions in Daniel 7, where the saints of the Most High are delivered into his hands for "a time, and times, and a half a time" (NASB), which would certainly correlate with the "time and times and half a time" (NASB) of Revelation 12:14.

Before we move on from this portion of Revelation and considering the persons and events of the tribulation, the one further area to consider briefly is the passage in Revelation 16, which delineates the seven bowl judgments. These seven bowls are described as containing the wrath of God, and are to be poured out upon the Earth, each by its respective angel. The most significant fact regarding these judgments is recorded several times, directly or indirectly, in the passage. That fact is that as a result of the judgments being poured out there is still no repentance on the part of those who are judged. Man still does not repent from his wickedness or acknowledge God's sovereignty and glory.

The first bowl is personal judgment upon the physical persons of those who have the mark of the beast, a "loathsome and malignant sore" (Rev. 16:2 NASB). The second bowl causes the death of every living thing in the sea, while the third bowl causes all fresh water streams to become blood. (Certainly this will completely disrupt the food chain, especially when we consider how much of the world's food is grown on irrigated ground).

The fourth bowl causes an increase in the intensity of the sun, causing men to be scorched by the fierce heat. It is interesting, once again, to note that the fears of environmentalists regarding "global warming" will be recognized here, not because of the acts of man, but because of God's direct intervention in the natural process for the purpose of bringing judgment. This is made clear by the judgment of the fifth bowl, which causes darkness throughout the world and yet the pain of the previous judgments does not diminish.

The sixth bowl causes the drying up of the Euphrates River to provide access to the Holy Land from the east. This is a preparatory judgment preceding the gathering of the nations for the Battle of Armageddon. The seventh bowl causes tremendous natural disasters, including thunder, lightning, earthquake, 100-pound hail, and destruction of islands and mountains. In addition, the destruction of cities is included in this judgment, including the city of Babylon, which we shall deal with separately.

The awesomeness of these great judgments is beyond our comprehension. When we read that "every island fled away, and the mountains were not found ... " (Rev. 16:20 NASB), it is beyond our ability to fathom. What is God doing here? Well perhaps, and this is mere speculation, but the climatic changes which took place at the time of the Flood, where the mountains were thrust up, may be changed as God's blessing comes to the Earth during the time of Christ's kingdom. Will this require the removal of the mountains and reshaping of continents? One cannot say with any degree of certainty, because God's Word does not contain this detail. But— and this is the most important fact seen in these bowl judgments—it is abundantly clear that these judgments are the outpouring of the wrath of God.

Revelation 16:1 makes this very clear in the command to the seven angels, "Go and pour out the seven bowls of the wrath of God into the earth" (NASB). Thank God that we who are believers in the Lord Jesus Christ as Savior have the promise that "God has not destined us for wrath, but for obtaining salvation through our Lord Jesus Christ" (1 Thess. 5:9 NASB).

CHAPTER ELEVEN

TEXT: MATTHEW 24; DANIEL 9–11; REVELATION 17–18

I n response to the question WHAT shall be the sign of Thy coming? Jesus replies by giving several signs that will portend His coming as King.

First, He cites (in Matt. 24:15) the necessity of the fulfillment of Daniel's prophecy found in Daniel 9:24–27. This prophecy, as Jesus emphasizes, speaks of the details of the intervening time between the time of Daniel and the time of the establishing of the Messianic kingdom, and particularly the covenant made by the Antichrist. Daniel's prophecy mentions several integral parts to the prophetic future (again, commencing from Daniel's time) of Israel:

1   To Daniel is revealed the fact that the "street ... and wall" (of Jerusalem) are to be "built in troublous times" (Dan. 9:25). This was fulfilled as recorded in the books of Ezra and Nehemiah.

2   The Messiah is to be "cut off" (Dan. 9:26). This was fulfilled at the time when Christ was crucified.

3   The city of Jerusalem is to be destroyed
     again. This was fulfilled in AD 70,
     when Titus sacked Jerusalem.

4   A covenant is confirmed and then
     broken. Since God does not break
     His promises (Heb. 6:17–18), this
     can speak of only one person who is
     to make a covenant with Israel, the
     Antichrist. In Matthew 24:15 the
     Lord makes reference to this breaking
     of the covenant.

But this information from the prophecy of Daniel
is incomplete without the further detail of the book of
Revelation. Further, in order to understand something
of the nature of the time and rule of the Antichrist,
it is helpful to understand something of the nature of
the political and religious system which will bring him
into power. Although it is not revealed in chronological
order, we will jump ahead to these chapters in the
book of Revelation in order to learn something of the
Antichrist and the influence of the system he represents.

Let us look at the political and religious system
which will bring the Antichrist into power. This system
is known as Babylon and it is described in detail in the
book of Revelation, as well as other prophetic Scriptures.
In looking at this description, it is important to see
that the system bears the characterization of an harlot
(Rev. 17:1–2, 15–16). This is the characterization in
Scripture, of one who knows the truth but refuses to

follow it "and they have played the harlot, departing from their God" (Hosea 4:12 NASB). In addition, the system is a leader in ecclesiastical affairs (Rev. 17:2, 5) and in political affairs (17:3). Further, the system has become very rich and influential (17:4), it represents something which has not been heretofore revealed in that it is called a mystery (17:5), it has been, historically, the great persecutor of the saints (17:6), and the system is an organized system of worldwide scope (17:15).

Significant also, in understanding the Antichrist and his influence, is an understanding of the history of Babylon. It was born out of human ambition against God (Gen. 11), and established as a counterfeit of God's plan of redemption. It was, and is, a "mystery religion" as described by Dr. Harry A. Ironside:

"The woman is a religious system, who dominates the civil power, at least for a time...we learn that the founder of Bab–el, or Babylon, was Nimrod, of whose unholy achievements we read in the 10th chapter of Genesis. He was the [one who] ... persuaded his associates and followers to join together in 'building a city and a tower which should reach unto heaven.' ... to be recognized as a temple or rallying center for those who did not walk in obedience to the word of the Lord. They called their city and tower Bab-El, the gate of God; but it was soon changed by divine judgment into Babel, Confusion. The wife of Nimrod was the infamous Semiramis the First. She is reputed to have been the foundress of the Babylonian mysteries and the

first high-priestess of idolatry. Thus Babylon became the fountainhead of idolatry, and the mother of every heathen and pagan system in the world. The mystery-religion that was there originated spread in various forms throughout the whole earth ... and is with us today...and shall have its fullest development when the Holy Spirit has departed and the Babylon of the Apocalypse holds sway." [26]

In explaining the deception which this Babylonian religion has brought into the religious systems of the world (and we must note here that we speak of religious systems, not of individuals within the systems who are always open to the miracle of God's grace), Ironside goes on to say:

"Building on the ... [biblical promise of Genesis 3:15] of the woman's Seed who was to come, Semiramis bore a son whom she declared was miraculously conceived! and when she presented him to the people, he was hailed as the promised deliverer. This was Tammuz, whose worship Ezekiel (in Ezekiel 8:14) protested against in the days of the captivity. Thus was introduced the mystery of the mother and the child, a form of idolatry that is older than any other known to man. The rites of this worship were secret. Only the initiated were permitted to know its mysteries. It was Satan's effort to delude mankind with an imitation so like the truth of God that they would not know the true Seed of the woman when He came in the fullness of time." [27]

Ironside continues to point out the fact that this image of the queen of heaven with the babe in her arms was seen everywhere, though the names might differ as languages differed. It became the mystery religion of the Phoenicians and Astoreth and Tammuz, the mother and child of these hardy adventures, became Isis and Horus in Egypt, Aphrodite and Eros in Greece, Venus and Cupid in Italy, and bore many other names in more distant places. Ironside goes on to say:

"Linked with this central mystery were countless lesser mysteries. Among these were the doctrines of purgatorial purification after death, salvation by countless sacraments such as priestly absolution, sprinkling with holy water, the offering of round cakes to the queen of heaven as mentioned in Jeremiah [7:18, 44:17, 18, 19, 25], dedication of virgins to the gods, which was literally sanctified prostitution, weeping for Tammuz for a period of 40 days, prior to the great festival of Ishtar, who was said to have received her son back from the dead; for it was taught that Tammuz was slain by a wild boar and afterwards brought back to life. To him the egg was sacred, as depicting the mystery of his resurrection, even as the evergreen was his chosen symbol and was set up in honor of his birth at the winter solstice, when a boar's head was eaten in memory of his conflict and a Yule-log burned with many mysterious observances. [What is universally considered as the]sign of the cross was sacred to Tammuz, as symbolizing the life-giving

principles and as the first letter of his name. It is represented upon vast numbers of the most ancient altars and temples, and did not, as many have supposed, originate with Christianity.

From this mystery-religion, the patriarch Abraham was separated by divine call; and with this same evil cult the nation that sprang from him was in constant conflict, until under Jezebel, a Phoenician princess, it was grafted onto what was left of the religion of Israel in the northern kingdom in the day of Ahab, and was the cause of their captivity at last. Judah was polluted by it, for Baal-worship was but the Canaanitish form of the Babylonian mysteries, and only by being sent into captivity to Babylon itself did Judah become cured of her fondness for idolatry. Baal was the Sun-God, the Life-giving One, identical with Tammuz. Though Babylon as a city had long been but a memory, her mysteries had not died with her. When the city and temples were destroyed, the high priest fled with a company if initiates and their sacred vessels and images to Pergamos, where the symbol of the serpent was set up as the emblem of the hidden wisdom. From there, they crossed the sea and emigrated to Italy ... where the ancient cult was propagated under the name of the Etruscan Mysteries, and eventually Rome became the headquarters of Babylonianism. The chief priests wore mitres shaped like the head of a fish, in honor of Dagon, the fish-god, the Lord of life – another form of the Tammuz mystery, as developed among Israel's old enemies, the Philistines. The chief priest when established in Rome took the title Pontifex Maximus, and this was imprinted on his mitre. When Julius Caesar (who, like all young Romans of good family, was an initiate) had become the head of the State, he was elected Pontifex Maximus, and this title was held henceforth by all the Roman emperors down to Constantine the Great, who was, at one and the same time, head of the church and high priest of the heathen! The title was afterwards conferred upon the bishops of Rome, and is borne by the pope today, who is thus declared to be, not the successor of the fisherman-apostle Peter, but the direct successor of the high priest of the Babylonian mysteries, and the servant of the fish-god Dagon, for whom he wears, like his idolatrous predecessors, the fisherman's ring." [28]

The passages in Daniel 11 describing the ruler of the end time after showing the progression of the history of the Grecian and Syrian empires and ultimately speaking of the Antichrist, gives confirmation to the alliances described above by Ironside. The prophecy of Daniel indicates that he "will honor a god of fortresses ... " (Dan. 11:38 NASB), with reference to his strong politico–religious alliances. However, to Daniel is also revealed the fact that his ultimate conflict will begin with the breakdown of this alliance, because "...rumors out of the East and the North shall trouble him ... "(Dan. 11:44). Viewing the geographical position of

Palestine, we realize that Babylon is to the east and Rome to the north. The political and religious alliance breaks down, Daniel prophesies, and this prophecy is confirmed by John's prophecy in Revelation 17:16. Why? "For God has put it in their hearts to execute His purpose by having a common purpose, and by giving their kingdom to the beast, until the words of God should be fulfilled" (NASB).

What does the Word of God indicate in Revelation 18 that the judgment of Babylon will be? The Beast, the Antichrist, who was dominated by the religious system of Babylon, rises against her and destroys her because it becomes apparent that she is in competition with the exclusive worship of the Antichrist. And so, the great counterfeit, which the author of confusion, the Devil himself, brought into existence to oppose God's plan of redemption, is ultimately brought to defeat and confusion from within. Once again, God's Word is proven true, a "house divided against itself cannot stand" (Matt. 12:25).

Having recognized that the fulfillment of Daniel's prophecy regarding the Antichrist is the first portion of Jesus' answer to his disciples question, and having taken the time to consider the religious and political system behind the rise to power of the Antichrist, let us now return to the additional factors in the Lord's answer to the disciples question. The Lord, secondly, delineates the events of the Great tribulation in verses 21–24. There will be: False prophets and false Christs coupled with great signs and wonders. It is important in this context and given the present climate in religion to note that miracles are not alone a proof of truth. This information is applicable in all periods of history and may help in evaluating televangelists and other "high profile" ministries, "If any one preach any other gospel ... let him be accursed" (Gal. 1:8).

Third, the Lord describes the fig tree putting forth leaves in verse 32. What is the fig tree? Notice that the disciples had just recently been involved in the Lord's action with a fig tree in Matthew 21:18–21. It would not be difficult to suppose, given their knowledge of the Old Testament, the comments the Lord had just made and prophecies He had referred to, that the disciples would make the connection between the fig tree which Jesus had cursed and the current and prophesied state of Israel, until it began to "revive" by putting on leaves.

Fourth, the Lord describes the "what" as to the signs of His coming in the terms of the "Days of Noah" syndrome. What were those of Noah's day taken away to? Quite clearly they were taken away to judgment, while Noah and his family remained. So, of the two in the field, and the two at the mill, the ones who are taken are symbolic of those who will be taken into judgment before Christ establishes His Kingdom. This concept of a judgment prior to the establishing of His Kingdom, the Lord will articulate further as He proceeds through this chapter and the next. But note particularly, that as He speaks of this event, He describes the slave who is evil, who thinks his master is delaying his coming, and because the slave is not prepared, he is "assigned" a place with the hypocrites, where "there will be weeping and gnashing of teeth" (Matt. 24:51). Note that the word "assign" used in this verse is also used in 2 Thessalonians 5:9 where it is translated "destined" and in John 15:16 where it is translated "appointed." Let the reader be reminded of the earlier premise established regarding the fact that not all who are a part of this Kingdom are believers. This becomes even more significant at this point!

CHAPTER TWELVE

TEXT: REVELATION 19–21

There are certain additional events of the tribulation upon which we must focus our attention. One has its beginning during the time that the events of the tribulation which we have seen are occurring, and the others are a part of the culmination of the tribulation.

First, there is an event described briefly in Revelation 19:7–10 known as the marriage supper of the Lamb. In looking at this event it will be helpful to note that the traditional Oriental wedding had three distinct parts , and these parts coincide directly with the events which are fulfilled in the life of the believer in the Lord Jesus Christ. They are:

First, the betrothal. Fulfilled when individuals believe.

Second, the coming through the streets for the bride, fulfilled at the rapture of the Church when Christ comes for the saints.

Third, the marriage. Fulfilled in heaven during the time that the tribulation is taking place on Earth, just before Christ comes back to Earth to reign. In the phrase "the marriage of the Lamb has come" (Rev. 19:7 NASB), the form "has come" designates a completed act. The marriage supper then follows the marriage and involves Israel.

In order to be sure that there is no misunderstanding of this truth, it will be helpful to answer these questions:

Who has been married? The answer, quite clearly from the evidence of the New Testament, is the Church. Such verses as John 3:29, "He that hath the bride is the bridegroom; but the friend of the bridegroom, who standeth and heareth him, rejoiceth greatly because of the bridegroom's voice; this my joy, therefore, is fulfilled." and 2 Corinthians 11:2, "for I have espoused you to one husband that I may present you as a chaste virgin to Christ." And Revelation 19:7–8, "[F]or the marriage of the Lamb is come, and his wife hath made herself ready. And to her was granted that she should be arrayed in fine linen, clean and white; for the fine linen is the righteousness of saints." Perhaps it is appropriate at this point to clarify that by the use of the term "Church" we mean all those who have become believers in the Lord Jesus Christ as Savior subsequent to His death, burial and resurrection, who have by faith in His shed blood been placed into His Body by the work of the Holy Spirit and who will be united with Him at His coming for His saints as foretold in 1 Thessalonians 4:18ff. These are, therefore, New Testament believers up to the time of the rapture, or the coming of Christ for His saints.

Where does this marriage take place? As we read the passage in Revelation 19, it becomes clear that it must take place in heaven, since it is from here that the righteous, those who are described earlier in the chapter as the wife, come with the King: "And the armies that were in heaven followed him upon white horses, clothed in fine linen, white and clean" (Rev. 19:14).

The Jewish wedding customs as they existed at the time of the writing of the New Testament, and many of which continue to this day, help us to understand the significance of the Marriage of the Lamb. Good gives these details:

"A young man went to the home of his potential bride-to-be. He carried three things with him: a large sum of money in order to pay the price for his bride, a betrothal contract called a "shitre erusin," and a skin of wine. Of course, anyone arriving with these things would immediately be under suspicion. The man approached the girl's father and older brothers. The contract was laid out, and the bride price was discussed. Finally, a glass of wine was poured. If the father approved, then the maiden was called in. If she also approved, then she would drink the wine. In doing so, she committed herself to this man, agreeing to follow the contract that now was a legal document between the two. They would be called husband and wife at this time, and their union could only be dissolved by a divorce. However, their status was that of betrothed, rather than that of fully married.

After the wine had been drunk, the man made the statement that he would go to his father's house and prepare a place for her. This place is known as the chadar (chamber), sometimes referred to as the chupah (or honeymoon bed). From the time that the shitre erusin was ratified, the young woman was consecrated, set apart, to her husband. She has been bought with a price. She must spend her time preparing to live as a wife and mother in Israel. Her days of waiting for her wedding are spent in learning how to please her husband.

Meanwhile, the young man returned to his father's home, and the chadar goes under construction. The room is provided with every comfort, as they will retire here for one week following their wedding ceremony. The young man, if asked when the day of his wedding will be, replies, "No man knows except my father." In Israel, the father had to be satisfied that every preparation had been made by his son before he gave him permission to go and get his bride. As at all weddings, focus was centered on the bride and groom. For this one day they were looked at as king and queen. Every effort was taken, and every possible expense was made to ensure their joy. On this day, tradition says, their sins are forgiven. They stand pure, without spot or blemish, as they are united."[29]

What a tremendous picture this is of all that the Lord taught and did while He was here on Earth. The passage in John 14:2 where He says that He is going "to prepare a place for you" certainly comes to mind as one reads of this Jewish custom. But more important to us is the concept of the commitment to the Bridegroom, as evidenced by the drinking of the wine–which He directed us to do "till He comes" (1 Cor. 11:26). With what great anticipation must the groom anticipate his father's words that the chamber is ready. Should not our anticipation be as great?

But now the question is, What about the marriage supper? It is an event that involves a restored and believing nation of Israel and takes place on the Earth. Matthew 22:1–14 is the familiar passage where the Lord describes the wedding supper. His teaching of this begins with the phrase, "The kingdom of heaven is like ... " Remember that earlier in this study we looked at the phrase "kingdom of heaven" in the book of Matthew, indicating that it was descriptive, most often, of the earthly millennial reign of Christ. Note now that in conjunction with the passage in Revelation 19, where the King is described as coming to Earth with his bride, the passage in Matthew begins to take on clearer meaning.

This is even more clear when Matthew 25:1–13, the parable of the virgins is added. We will see in chapter 14 that the virgins speak clearly of Israel, God's earthly people, the friend of the bridegroom and bride, who will celebrate the wedding at the marriage supper of the Lamb. We do not have complete information in Scripture regarding the exact timing of this event, but clearly it occurs in conjunction with the coming of the Bridegroom, the return of the Lord Jesus Christ to Earth, and probably is the first event of the millennium, especially when consideration is given to the event next considered, that immediately on the King's return there is a war to be won.

This brings us to the second major event covered in this passage, which is the Battle of Armageddon, the event which culminates the time of the tribulation. It is characterized by four distinct features. First, it is described in Old Testament prophecies as a gathering of " ... all the nations" (Zech. 14:2ff. See also Isa. 34:2; 63:3; Ezek. 38–39; Joel 3). Second, it is to be the last phase in a final and complete judging of Israel. Zechariah 14:1 indicates this when the prophet Zechariah says, "Behold, the day of the Lord cometh, and thy spoil shall be divided in the midst of thee."

Third, it is to be the time of deliverance by the Lord of believing Israel, as Zechariah goes on to indicate, "And ye shall flee to the valley of the mountains... and the Lord, my God, shall come, and all the saints with thee" (Zech. 14:5). Fourth, it is to be a time of judgment against the nations who have been enemies of Israel, "And this shall be the plague with which the Lord will smite all the peoples that have fought against Jerusalem ... " (Zech. 14:12). It is important to note, as the apostle John describes the event in Revelation 16:13–16 and in Revelation 19:17–21, that the battle is between those forces which are gathered together by the demons which proceed from the dragon, the beast, and the false prophet (Rev. 16:13), and the one who sits upon a white horse and "is called Faithful and True" (Rev. 19:11), against whom these armies are "gathered together to make war against him that sat on the horse, and against his army" (Rev. 19:19).

The third major event in this passage is the inauguration of the millennium—the kingdom of heaven—Christ's kingdom. Four questions are answered in relation to this period of time in the passage before us in Revelation and in the related passages. The first question is, Where does this kingdom occur? And the answer is on Earth, as prophesied throughout Scripture and emphasized by such passages as Zechariah 14:4: "And his feet shall stand in that day upon the Mount of Olives, which is before Jerusalem on the east ... " There are some who would attempt to make this kingdom a heavenly or spiritual kingdom, but to do so one must accept a non-literal hermeneutic, because quite clearly if this is not a literal kingdom, then several things prophesied by Zechariah cannot be. If the kingdom is not on Earth, then Zechariah is clearly mistaken because it cannot really be His feet that stand. It cannot be on a given day, it cannot be that He really stands on the Mount of Olives and it cannot really be Jerusalem!

Each of these literally described things must be spiritualized in some way to make the kingdom of heaven a spiritual and not an earthly kingdom. To do this calls into question other key hermeneutical principles of Old Testament prophecy; one of the key ones being was the Messiah to be born of a virgin? Did Christ ever literally come to Earth the first time, or was this story of His incarnation merely a spiritual lesson rather than a literal truth? The answer sometimes given to this argument is that the first advent can be proven from history, and that is true. But that argument would have been of little value to Simeon. His confidence was in the literal truth of God's Word regarding a coming Savior, and for this his faith was rewarded (Luke 2:25–35).

May God grant that our faith in His Word may be as strong. God in His Sovereign wisdom has given us sufficient detail in verses such as this that we cannot overlook them. In addition, as we see the one thousand years mentioned in Revelation 20, verses 2, 4, and 7, we note that the devil is first bound at the beginning of this time and at the end is loosed, gathers the nations to battle and they come up "on the breadth of the earth, and compassed the camp of the saints about ... " (Rev. 20:9). The obvious question is, How could they compass the camp of the saints if these saints were not on Earth? Clearly, the saints are with the king, for the verses immediately preceding in chapter 19 of Revelation (19:14) have so indicated. The king and the kingdom are on Earth.

The second question regarding this kingdom is, When does it occur? It is now clear from the chronology which John gives us in these chapters in Revelation, as well as the chronology which the Lord Himself has also given us in Matthew 24 and 25, that the millennial kingdom occurs following the tribulation, the Battle of Armageddon, and the judgment of the sheep and the goats.

The third question is, How long does it last? One thousand years is the indication given to us by the apostle John in Revelation 20:2, 4, and 7, as we have already noted. There are some who have taught that this is merely a metaphor; a figure of speech to indicate an extended kingdom and that this is, in reality, the ushering in of the eternal kingdom. Perhaps the clearest argument against this, in the mind of this writer, is the fact that the temple to be rebuilt at Jerusalem is described by the Lord as "the place of My throne and the place of the soles of My feet, where I will dwell among the sons of Israel forever" (Ezek. 43:7).

What does this mean? In this verse in Ezekiel, as well as in several other verses within the same context in Ezekiel, the promise is made that, "My dwelling place also will be with them; and I will be their God, and they will be My people ... when My sanctuary is in their midst forever" (Ezek. 37:28–29 NASB). Is this the heavenly kingdom? Certainly the term "forever," standing by itself would indicate that, but it does not stand by itself. It is qualified by the passage which follows describing a temple and city with precise measurements which do not match the measurements of the city in Revelation 21 and in which there is no temple because, quite simply, in Revelation 20:22 John says, "And I saw no temple in it, for the Lord God, the Almighty, and the Lamb, are its temple" (NASB).

What is happening? There is here, as often in prophecy, a look beyond a single event. Clearly, the physical measurements of a city and temple relate to the "kingdom of heaven," the Messianic kingdom of Christ on Earth, while the advent of that kingdom is the fulfillment of God's promises to His people, which will mean that from that point on, for the one thousand years of the millennium and on into the eternity of the new heaven, new earth and new Jerusalem God will dwell with His people forever, but the earthly kingdom need not be eternal for those prophecies to be fulfilled, and cannot be if all is to be taken as it is written.

In discussing the issue of the literal earthly kingdom, Dr. Feinberg says this:

"No other reasonable interpretation can possibly be given to the plain words: "and they lived and reigned with Christ a thousand years." In the second place, the millennial reign spoken of is to take place on earth. In Revelation 5:10 the redeemed and the four living ones sing a new song which contains the words: "and we shall reign on the earth." Amos predicted that God would raise up the tabernacle of David and "build it as in the days of old." In the days of old, if the Scriptures mean what they say, the tabernacle of David was on earth. Furthermore, when the seventh angel sounded the trumpet, the great voices in heaven declared anticipatively: "The kingdoms of this world [mark you, it is not of heaven, but of this world] are become the kingdoms of our Lord, and of his Christ; and he shall reign for ever and ever." In the third place, the passage is directly connected with the second coming of Christ. The last verses of the nineteenth chapter record the coming to earth of the Lord Jesus Christ, so there is no necessity of mentioning the fact once more in the twentieth chapter. There is no flaw whatsoever in the chronology of John." [30]

How is this peaceful kingdom to be accomplished? The passage before us in Revelation makes it clear that the influence of the adversary is eliminated by "binding Satan" for one thousand years in the bottomless pit. In addition, Revelation 19:15, and 20:1-3, in conjunction with such Old Testament passages as Isaiah 11:4 and

Zechariah 14:9–19, indicates that the rule of this kingdom will be with a "rod of iron" over the nations, enforcing the worship of the Messiah and the leadership of His people, Israel.

The fourth major event described in the passage before us is the time known as the Day of God. The apostle Peter describes this in 2 Peter 3:12 when he says, "Looking for and hastening the coming of the day of God, on account of which the heavens will be destroyed by burning, and the elements will melt with intense heat!" (NASB). Revelation 20:9 describes this event in succinct detail following a description of the nations being gathered by the devil and his emissaries against the camp of the saints when it says, " ... and fire came down from heaven and devoured them."

Included in the time of the Day of God is the fifth major event, the great white throne judgment, in which all the dead are judged "according to their deeds" (Rev. 20:13). It is important to note this judgment in relation to what has already been discussed regarding the judgments recorded in Scripture. This is the carrying out of the sentence already determined as a result of a choice made at the time of crisis, the hour of decision, by the individuals involved. Notice that, as the unbeliever so often describes the final judgment as the weighing up of the good against the bad, these who stand at this judgment are judged by their deeds. How can that be? Because of the words of Scripture, "All our righteousnesses are as filthy rags" (Isa. 64:6). God allows the deeds to be examined, and man is proven guilty because of those deeds, that "...every mouth may be stopped, and all the world may become guilty before God" (Rom. 3:19).

Finally, the passage before us deals with the ushering in of the new heaven, the new earth and the new Jerusalem. Little is given us of descriptive information regarding the eternal state, except to tell us that we will be with our Savior, Jesus Christ, " ... that where I am, there ye may be also" (John 14:3), and the description in the final chapters of Revelation which describe the incredible beauty and holiness of this, our eternal abode.

CHAPTER THIRTEEN

TEXT: MATTHEW 13:31–35, 41–52

There are six remaining parables in Matthew 13, each of which teaches us a distinctive characteristic of the kingdom of heaven.

The first is the parable of the mustard seed (Matt. 13:31–32), and the significant details of this parable as given by our Lord are these: an insignificant beginning, phenomenal growth (probably 9 to 12 feet was the height of the plant to which Jesus was referring), and the "birds of the air" who nest in the branches.

Note that these birds nest in the branches, but are not branches. This is something which has occurred throughout Scripture where God is dealing with His people. There has always been a "mixed multitude," a "throng," made up of those who are interested spectators but not believers. Quite often this group is responsible for undermining the faith of God's people and making them discontent with that which God has provided, and also responsible, from the human standpoint, for detracting some from becoming believers (Matt. 13:4; Gen. 40:17, 19; Jer. 5:27; Rev. 18:2).

The second parable is the parable of the leaven in the measures of meal (Matt. 13:33). Again, there are certain significant features which describe the Kingdom of Heaven, the Lord says. "The kingdom of heaven is like ... " are His words, and then He proceeds to describe the measures of meal as the beginning.

Next, leaven is added to this meal. Leaven in Scripture is always typical of that which is evil and nowhere represents good (Ex. 12:15, 19; Lev. 2:11; Matt. 16:6, 12; Mark 8:15; Luke 12:1; 1 Cor. 5:6–9; Gal. 5:9). From one's perspective in this day and age, one often does not catch the significance of the fact that leaven is typical of sin. That is because one goes to the supermarket refrigerator case and purchases a wrapped packet of dry yeast, which is used for leavening. Or perhaps the contact is even more limited, bread and rolls are purchased already prepared!

The leaven of Scripture is in the sourdough tradition, that which is in the process of decay, a portion of each batch of bread dough is preserved until the next preparation. It is sour because it is in the process of souring! It is souring because it is decaying. What causes decay? The curse of sin, and thus leaven by its very nature typifies the process which each human is undergoing, and which all of creation is undergoing as a result of the Fall.

The Lord goes on to say that, "The whole is leavened ... " the entire domain is permeated. Many have likened this to the proclamation of the gospel throughout the world. Would that the gospel had permeated the world. Certainly, as a devotional thought, we may make an application of this type on cursory examination of the passage, but Scripture does not uphold an interpretation of this passage in this way, because it would require a realignment of all that Scripture has taught regarding leaven.

The question one has to ask is this: Did the Master Teacher, the Lord Jesus Christ, the living Word of God, know what Scripture taught? Of course He did. Though finite teachers might draw inadequate or erroneous analogies, would the Perfect One? No! Thus, the interpretation must indicate a gradual permeating of the earthly kingdom of the Messiah by those who are unregenerate. It is for this reason that the kingdom culminates in judgment against the unbelievers as seen so clearly in Revelation 20:7–9.

There is a tremendously important comment, and many have treated it as a passing comment, which the Scripture makes at this point. Notice that it is here that Matthew, under the supervision of the Holy Spirit, quotes from the psalmist and says, "I will utter things kept secret from the foundations of the world" (Matt. 13:35 NASB). These are new truths which Jesus is teaching, and the hearers and readers do well to recognize them as such. They will not be contained in old wineskins, nor will they fit into the warp and woof of the old garments. Would to God that theologians throughout church history had recognized this as the apostle Paul did, and had taught the mystery "which in other generations was not made known to the sons of men, as it has now been revealed to His holy apostles and prophets in the Spirit; to be specific, that the Gentiles are fellow heirs and fellow members of the body, and fellow partakers of the promise in Christ Jesus through the gospel" (Eph. 3:5–6 NASB).

Specifically, the Lord Jesus is teaching a distinction between the Kingdom of God (all believers in the Lord Jesus Christ as Savior from all ages), and the earthly kingdom of the Messiah. Heretofore, the only understanding that had been imparted was limited, and it appeared that Israel was God's sole plan and purpose. Now there is indication of a future for Israel, in an earthly kingdom as promised, but also additional new truth.

The third parable is that of the treasure in the field, found in Matthew 13:44. Notice the pertinent details. It is hidden to all but one. It required a purchase of the field—which is the world. Remember the earlier interpretation which the Lord gave? Before further comment on this is made, let the reader proceed directly to the fourth parable and comment will be made on them by contrasting them.

The fourth parable is the parable of the Pearl found in Matthew 13:45–46. Note that it is found by one person again. Note also, that it too required a purchase, but not of the ocean, but the pearl. This purchase is typical of the Church, the body of Christ, purchased out of the world, whereas the treasure in the field is typical of the nation Israel, purchased in the world. (For further discussion of this teaching, see chapter fifteen dealing with Matthew 25:14–30 and the discussion on Israel and the Church as God's possessions).

The fifth parable is the parable of the dragnet found in Matthew 13:47–50. It describes a net cast into the sea, which when drawn out of the sea is found to contain both good and bad. At this point it is important to note that this parable can in no way speak of the Church which is the body of Christ. Church historians, from as far back as St. Augustine, in attempting to justify the "territorial" church, whether it be Roman Catholic, Lutheran, Reformed, Anglican, or whatever, have interpreted this parable to indicate that it typifies the church, showing that the church in its territory contains both righteous and unrighteousness. What is the criteria for determining interpretation? The Scripture above all else. The Word of God says this, "If any man have not the Spirit of Christ, he is none of His" (Rom. 8:4b). No matter what church historians have said, we must recognize that each one is a product of his particular background and pressing needs of his time. In every case we must "search the Scripture to see whether those things are so" (Acts 17:11). Therefore, it is abundantly clear from Scripture that a member of the Church is one and only one who has been made a part of the body of Christ through faith in His shed blood.

Finally, with regard to this parable, note that the separating is done by the angels – not by the Lord. We refer again to our comment on the parable of the wheat and the tares.

The sixth parable is the parable of the scribe found in Matthew 13:51–52. He is, as would be known by the listeners to the Lord Jesus, one who is instructed in the Word of God, that is, specifically, the Old Testament, since that was the written word that existed at that time. The Lord goes on to describe him as being like one who "brings out of his treasure things new and old." What treasure did a scribe have? His knowledge of and immersion in the Scripture were his treasure. He is described as bringing out of that treasure things old, signifying the Old Testament which he had been taught, and now new truths which Jesus is teaching. Again, this is a significant emphasis, not by the interpreter, but by the Teacher, on the contrast between old and new.

CHAPTER FOURTEEN

TEXT: MATTHEW 25:31–46, 1–13; DANIEL 12

I t will be most helpful , before proceeding further with our study in Matthew 25, to take the time to review the various judgments that are mentioned in Scripture. Often, as a result of our hymnody and reciting of credal statements, we do not distinguish amongst these judgments which are defined clearly and distinctly in Scripture. And so, let us review, without any attempt to place them in order as they are introduced in Scripture, but in a more chronological order as they are dealt with in the life of the believer or in the chronology of historical and prophetic events.

First, the judgment of the world as indicated in John 12:31: "Now judgment is upon this world; now the ruler of this world shall be cast out" (NASB). This judgment speaks of the condemnatory sentence passed upon the world system, governed by Satan, in that it is convicted of wickedness, and its power broken. It is also very closely related, because both are related to the work of Christ on the cross to the judgment of sinners taught in John 3:19 by the Lord Jesus. When speaking to Nicodemus, He said, "And this is the judgment, that the light is come into the world, and men loved the darkness rather than the light; for their deeds were evil" (NASB). The word used in John 3:19 in the Greek is the word *krisis* (*crisis*) from which, quite obviously, our English word crisis is transliterated. It denotes the act of distinguishing and separating which may be done by another, as in a judge or jury making a decision as to whether a person is innocent or guilty, or may be done by oneself in identifying oneself with one side or another. Thus, the judgment of sinners is that sentence which is passed when men refuse to follow the light revealed to them so as to come to a knowledge of the truth (Rom. 1:19) and thus by their own actions come into the state of a condemned one. This is the precise reason for the judgment of the world system and the ruler thereof, who by his own actions came into the state of the condemned.

The second judgment is the judgment of believers taught in 1 Corinthians 11:31, "But let a man examine himself, and so let him eat of that bread and drink of that cup .... " The word here translated *examine* is again the same word as above, the word *crisis,* or the act of distinguishing and separating. It is used in the New Testament of believers only when it is self-imposed, that is, when the believer examines himself, or comes to a time of crisis in his life so as to face the sin and confess it in order to escape the discipline of the Lord

The third judgment is The Judgment of Israel as taught in such passages as Ezekiel 20:33–38 which speaks of Israel "passing under the rod." The word used in the Septuagint is the word *aforizo*, which means to separate, from which we get our English word *horizon*, that which separates the seen from the unseen. This judgment, or separation, occurs during the time of the Day of the Lord, the time of the re-gathering for that judgment that Ezekiel describes, the time which the Lord describes as the time of tribulation. It is a separation of believing Israel from unbelieving Israel.

The fourth biblical judgment is the judgment of angels mentioned in Jude 6: "And the angels who kept not their first estate, but left their own habitation, he hath reserved in everlasting chains under darkness unto the judgment of the great day." (See also 2 Pet. 2:4). Again the word used here is the word indicating a crisis. The crisis occurred when the angels sinned, and though sentence has been passed, the judgment has not been executed. This principle is important to understand in relation to much that God does and allows in the world today with regard to Satan. Judgment has not yet been carried out, though the sentence has been passed. Wickedness is allowed to continue even though the sentence has been passed in order that others might believe the gospel.

The fifth judgment is the judgment of the sheep and the goats taught by our Lord Jesus in Matthew 25:32ff. We shall cover this in greater detail later in this chapter, and will only mention the fact here that the word *aforizwo*, a separation, is the operative word in regard to this judgment.

The sixth judgment is the judgment of the great white throne as delineated in Revelation 20:11–15. At this great white throne are gathered all the dead, those who are not recorded in the book of life. The dead are judged, and the word here is a different word than used in the other judgments, it is the word *krino* from the noun *krima* from which we get our word *crime*.[31] This word is used in a way which indicates to pronounce an opinion concerning right and wrong and is used throughout the New Testament to indicate the act of Jesus Christ, as the appointed Judge, in determining the righteousness or unrighteousness of those who stand before the throne. A crime is stated as having occurred and the judgment of guilty is passed. Note once again that it is the dead who stand here. The living are in heaven!

The seventh judgment indicated in Scripture is the judgment seat of Christ as taught in 2 Corinthians 5:10: "For we must all appear before the judgment seat of Christ .... " The word translated *judgment* here is the word *bema*, which denotes a place where those come for hearing who because of their citizenship have rights and standing with the court. It is used in Scripture, as well as in secular Greek literature of the time, as the place of determining of reward or lack thereof, not a place of retribution or condemnation. Perhaps the clearest picture of this, since the word means "a step or raised place or platform,"[32] is the picture which we have in modern times of the athlete who has competed in the Olympic Games who, in order to receive his reward, steps onto the raised platform to receive the appropriate recognition for his achievement.

Having completed this review of biblical judgments, let us now note that as the Lord continues His response to the disciples questions, He has moved on from a discussion of what and when, to a far reaching consideration of who. There are three ways in which Christ explains the means of determining who will enter the kingdom of heaven.

The way in which Christ explains the means of entry into His earthly kingdom is by His teaching about the judgment of the sheep and the goats. We can best understand this particular judgment by asking several pertinent questions. The first is, Who is present? And the answer is quite simple. There are sheep, there are goats, and there are brethren. Perhaps the reader will readily see the first two, but the third group is distinguished by the words of the Lord, "...these my brethren," which he repeats several times in the passage. This truth is emphasized in the passage which we have previously quoted from Daniel 12:1 regarding the rescue of Daniel's people from the "time of distress" because their "names are written in the book." (See below for further explanation).

So, the next logical question is, Who are the sheep? For the answer to this one we must go somewhat afield from this passage, and look at the passages in Revelation which describe the events of the tribulation and time leading into the Messianic kingdom. When we do that, we discover that the sheep are those who have believed the "gospel of the kingdom" and have not been martyred. Because the "gospel of the kingdom" is preached in all nations (Matt. 24:14) there will be many who believe, "a great company which no man can number" (Rev. 7:9) will be martyred, but logistics and certainly God's gracious intervention will apparently limit the ability of the Antichrist to destroy all those who believe. These are "saints" by faith in the shed blood of Christ who have "repent[ed], for the kingdom of heaven is at hand" and to whom is given the possession of the kingdom as promised in Daniel 7:22. These are definitely Gentiles–note that the word translated "nations" is the word *eqnos*, (*ethnos*, from which the English word *ethnic* originates), and is translated 93 times in the King James Version, and similarly in other accepted translations as *Gentiles*; 5 times as *heathen*; 64 times as *nations*; and twice as *people* (Luke 2:32; Matt. 4:15; Acts 13:46; Acts 14:2; Gal. 2:15; Acts 2:5; Rom. 1:5; Gal. 3:8; Joel 3:2, 12, 14). Who are the goats? Again, because they are not brethren they are of the Gentiles and are those who have not believed of Gentile nations.

Who are the brethren? Given the events which the Lord has described, and understanding that Israel, the "brethren" according to the flesh of the Messiah, that nation Israel—the people of the king—are the only ones who could truly be, under these circumstances, the brethren of the king. These are those who have most recently been "stranger[s], naked, hungry, sick, and in prison ... " (v. 38) because of the "time of sorrow," the tribulation they have just experienced–clearly they are those who have been sealed to pass through this time of tribulation, the 144,000 who have experienced being strangers whom these Gentile believers (sheep) have protected.

How are the sheep and goats separated? Notice this, because it is critical to the true understanding of the judgment. This is not, as some have supposed, a delineation of righteous nations, or, as it were, flocks of sheep, but these are divided "As a shepherd divideth the sheep from the goats ... " (v. 32)–one by one is the only way in which this can be done, and certainly was the way in which it was done in the time of the giving of this description. (Remember that the village fold, the common fold used by all the shepherds of the village when they were not out in the desert feeding their sheep, was a fold in which all of the village flocks were kept, and for which a porter (John 10:3) was given charge. The shepherd then came to the door of the fold and called out "his own sheep by name" (John 10:3), separating them from the goats as they were called out).

At the beginning of this chapter it was noted that all judgments in Scripture which involve death also involve individual accountability. This judgment clearly prescribes some to death, and thus God, who is ever and infinitely Just and Immutable, carries out this judgment in the same and unchanging way that He does all other judgments, on an individual basis.

How does one know the brethren are Israel and sheep and goats are Gentiles? This question is answered by going back in the account to the parable of the ten virgins. Who are the virgins? Are they the Church? Some have taught that they are. Some questions must be answered if this is the case. Who is the Bridegroom?

If, as the Scripture seems to clearly indicate, the Lord Jesus is the Bridegroom (John 3:29), then who is the bride? The bride of Christ is taught clearly throughout the New Testament as being the Church (Eph. 5:25–27). If the Church is the bride, then who are the friends who are described as the virgins. Remember that in the tradition of the Oriental wedding, the ceremony had taken place, and the bridegroom is now coming with his bride through the streets of the city to the wedding feast, to which the friends are invited. These are clearly not the Church. The Church is the one who returns with the Bridegroom as His bride. Are they Gentiles then? Probably not, because of the significance of the number 10. Often the number 10 refers, when speaking to the Jewish audience, of the 10 tribes of Israel, that portion of the divided kingdom whose loyalty to the king was not certain. Judah is always typified as God's chosen ones (Gen. 49:8–12) while Israel as a separate kingdom (10 tribes) is typical of the people's rejection of God (see 2 Kings 17:20–23). The ten virgins are typical of Israel during the tribulation, some of whom believe and are therefore found with oil (type of the Holy Spirit throughout Scripture) and others who do not, as throughout the Old Testament Israel is a mixed multitude. It is important to note here, as well, that the passage in Revelation 14:3–4, which is speaking of the 144,000, describes them as those who "have not been defiled with women, for they have kept themselves chaste." Virgins are again, therefore, identified as those of Israel who are faithful believers in the Lord.

Now comes the separation spoken of in Ezekiel 20:37. What is the basis of their entry into the wedding feast? Whether they are known to the Lord or not (verse 12) and whether they have the light (John 8:12). Thus it is clear that these who are described as virgins are those in Revelation 14:4, who are believers, "followers" of the Lamb, "purchased from among men." This truth is emphasized clearly by reference to the prophet whom the Lord Himself refers the disciples to, the prophet Daniel. In Daniel 12:1 are these words, "and there will be a time of distress such as never occurred since there was a nation until that time."

Note how close these words are to the words of the Lord in Matthew 24:21, "For then there will be a great tribulation, such as has not occurred since the beginning of the world until now, nor ever shall" (NASB), "and at that time your people, everyone who is found written in the book, will be rescued" (NASB). Those who are "written in the book," the believers, are rescued, and enter the kingdom. Notice also, that the time of this distress is described to Daniel in response to his question, "How long will it be to the end of these wonders?" (Dan. 12:6 NASB) as "a time, times and half a time, and as soon as they finish shattering the power of the holy people, all these events will be completed" (Daniel 12:7 NASB). Remember, also, our discussion regarding the marriage supper of the Lamb, which was seen as occurring at the close of the Tribulation as the initial event of the millennial kingdom, and note that those friends, the wise virgins, are admitted to the wedding feast.

There is one further factor spoken of to Daniel in relation to this time of tribulation and the ultimate establishing of the kingdom of the Son of Man. To Daniel is given the revelation that there will be a resurrection of the righteous (Dan. 12:3) at the end of the tribulation in which he will be included, because the final verse of the book of Daniel contains this promise directed to the faithful prophet, "But as for you, go your way to the end; then you will enter into rest and rise again for your allotted portion at the end of the age" (Daniel 12:13 NASB).

Notice the promise of resurrection and the phrase which was used by the disciples in their original question in Matthew 24:3, "the end of the age." Clearly, this was a phrase understood by Daniel and by the disciples, and to which they looked forward with hope and comfort.

CHAPTER FIFTEEN

TEXT: MATTHEW 25:14–30

This passage is most significant in the truths which the Lord is making known to His disciples, as it clearly is the crux of the entire discourse given by our Lord, which discourse is a response to the disciples' questions:

"When shall these things be?"

"What shall be the sign of Thy coming?"

"What shall be the sign of the end of the age?"

The answers to these questions are reiterated in these verses. Read and study them carefully!

In examining this passage, the first question to ask is, Who are the characters? The first person presented to us is the master of the household. There is no clear definition of who he is, nor is there a clear definition of the household of which he is the master. But he clearly has power beyond the ordinary master. See verse 30 where he prescribes the punishment for the unworthy servant as "outer darkness, there will be weeping and gnashing of teeth." The next characters presented to us are the slaves. It is important to note that they are not merely hired servants. The word translated slave denotes ownership as a result of a purchase.[33]

After discovering the characters who are introduced, one should then ask the question, What is the responsibility which is given by the master to each slave? This can be answered quite succinctly from the passage. Each slave is expected to be a good steward of that which is entrusted to the slave, and to give an account upon the master's return.

What is there to learn from this passage, and from other passages which deal with judgment as to stewardship? First, as one examines the concept of the slaves as "owned ones," those who have been purchased with a price, one remembers that the Scripture teaches very clearly that God has purchased two distinct groups of people to be His. He has purchased the nation Israel to be His people as taught in the Old Testament and made clear in Leviticus 26:12 and the verses following. He has also purchased the Church as the body and bride of Christ, as taught in 1 Corinthians 6:20, and Ephesians 1:3 and 2:10.

Second, one also learns in conjunction with the principle of purchase and ownership, that two distinct groups are called "elect" in the Scripture. The nation Israel is called God's elect in such verses as Isaiah 45:4, and so also is the Church in such passages as 1 Peter 1:2. The writer is aware that some will make no distinction between these two groups, but the reader should refer to the clear distinction made throughout Scripture indicating that God is able to distinguish between His people Israel as God's elect, and those of all races and nations who are also His elect "according to the foreknowledge of God the Father, by the sanctifying work of the Spirit, that you may obey Jesus Christ and be sprinkled with His blood ... " (1 Pet. 1:2). It is interesting to note, as somewhat an aside to the subject, but in regard to the elect of God, that Christ is also referred to in both Old Testament and New Testament as God's elect (Isa. 42:1; 1 Pet. 2:6).

Third, one learns that one group of individuals will be judged for their works and yet still saved because of their faith. This group is presented to us in 1 Corinthians 3. The apostle Paul describes in this chapter the appearing at the bema seat those who have built upon the foundation of Jesus Christ. As their works are evaluated, Paul makes the statement that for those whose works do not stand the test, the works will be consumed and "yet he himself shall be saved, yet so as by fire" (1 Cor. 3:15). Why can he say that? Because they are part of a group whose access into the group is determined by individual faith. Please note that the writer said access into the group; that is, identification as a part of a particular group, not access into heaven. Access into heaven is always as a result of individual faith as stated clearly in John 3:3, which the members of this group clearly have. They are distinguished from some of the other groups who are also believers by faith who do not appear at this bema seat.

Fourth, another group of individuals will be judged for their works, and some will be cast into torment as seen in Matthew 25:30. Why is this group different from the group above? Because even though they are part of a group who are "God's people" they have, as individuals, not ever exercised any personal faith in the Messiah, the Master, the Lord Jesus Christ. Thus they are a part of a particular group whose access into the group is not determined by, nor identified by, their individual faith, resulting in new birth, but rather they are part of a group determined by natural birth, that is, they are part of the nation Israel. As has always been true in God's economy, access into heaven is not determined by natural birth, but through new birth as a result of individual faith.

Fifth, , access into the true family of God is therefore always by personal faith in the Lord Jesus Christ as Savior, and that faith, once exercised, is sealed by the Holy Spirit and the "inheritance" is guaranteed (Eph. 1:13–14), and the believer "shall not come into judgment, but is passed from death into life" (John 5:24 NASB).

So, the Lord is teaching that those who are seen in this passage are those who are held accountable by the Master, they are those who are owned by the Master as His chosen earthly people, they have been entrusted with specific wealth and responsibility, and, upon the Master's return, they are held to account. Those who have not served in accordance with the Master's instructions are cast into torment. These do not pass the test when "passing under the rod" (Ezek. 20:37), because they are Israelites outwardly but:

"[H]e is not a Jew who is one outwardly; neither is circumcision that which is outward in the flesh. But he is a Jew who is one inwardly; and circumcision is that which is of the heart, by the Spirit, not by the letter; and his praise is not from men, but from God" (NASB).

This is the point of decision. For those of you who are reading this who are committed to the teaching of the "perseverance of the saints," as John Calvin expressed it, you cannot have it two (or even three) ways! Either you must admit that there is a clear distinction between the Kingdom of God (in which all who have accepted the work of the Lord Jesus Christ on their behalf, whether as a future promise or a past reality are, through that faith, made a permanent part of God's family) and the literal earthly kingdom of the Lord Jesus Christ as Messiah (in which some who are owned as God's people are nevertheless sent into outer darkness) or you must admit that some who are God's people do not persevere! The only other alternative (the third way), is to deny that the Lord Jesus as the Perfect One knew what He was teaching, and claim that His words and His Word cannot be believed with confidence since His analogies might not always hold true.

If the Lord Jesus Christ was the perfect God and perfect Man in His incarnation, and therefore the perfect Teacher, the question is this: Did He know and understand what He was teaching? And did He teach it without error, express or implied? One must believe this to have any true basis for his or her faith. If we cannot have confidence in this, our entire faith is only in our own judgment, we must, with the neo-orthodox position, claim that the Word of God is only inspired when it "speaks to us."[34]

Many have asked this writer, "Why does it make any difference what we believe about the tribulation, or the millennium?" The inference from this question is often that it is merely something to "be divisive" about. That is not the case, and certainly those who are orthodox and dispensational in their position on the inspiration and interpretation of God's Word will have much to answer for in this regard, because we have not been faithful in making the issue clear.

The issue is not whether you agree with some human author or speaker; the issue is whether you believe God's Word and can have confidence that God is unchangeable. If He is unchangeable, then He does not send to punishment those who are His own people who are believers in the work of the Lord Jesus Christ, because His Word clearly promises that those believers "will not come into judgment, but [are] passed from death into life" (John 5:24). But He does, on the other hand, just as emphatically promise that those who are of His people Israel, as well as all others who have refused to hear His Son and believe in Him, have been "condemned" (Rom. 3:9).

And so, the issue is not, what about the kingdom, or the tribulation, the issue is, what about God's Word? Can we believe what it says, or does it require some special insight or interpretation not available to every believer in Christ? The Word of God clearly states that it is not of any "private interpretation" (2 Peter 1:20), but that the Holy Spirit is both the Author and Interpreter. We can have confidence that God's Word is addressed to us, it is its own best commentator, and it is given that we may "know the truth" (John 8:32).

CHAPTER SIXTEEN

TEXT: REVELATION 20:4–6; DANIEL 12; MATTHEW 24:27–51, 25:1–46

W hat will occur during the earthly reign of the Lord Jesus Christ and why is this period of time so important as to delay the unveiling of the new heaven and the new earth? To answer this question it will be helpful to look at the millennium in the same way as was done with the tribulation, considering the nature, the source, and the purpose of the messianic kingdom.

The **nature of the millennium** is made clear in the teaching of the Lord Jesus in the passage before us in Matthew. In the teaching of the Lord it is clear from the contrast between the faithful slave of Matthew 24:45 who is put in charge of the household and who, on his master's return is found faithfully discharging that duty and the "evil" slave whose attitude is described by his statement in verse 48, "My master is not coming for a long time ... " and whose judgment is to be assigned "a place with the hypocrites; weeping shall be there and the gnashing of teeth" (Matt. 24:51 NASB).

That, on the one hand, is the response of faith, which produces righteousness, on the other hand is the judgment of hell. This clearly indicates that those who enter the earthly kingdom of the Messiah are righteous, those who have believed in the good news of the kingdom. As we have already seen in looking at the time of tribulation, God's purpose in bringing about that time of judgment is to purify His people.

The teaching of the Lord Jesus in the subsequent passages confirms this. We have already seen that the five foolish virgins, those who do not have the oil, are left out as those whom the Bridegroom does not know (Matt. 25:12). In the same manner, as we have seen, those servants to whom talents are entrusted are rewarded for their faithfulness, and to the unfaithful, eternal punishment. As was noted in that study, there cannot be the righteousness of God's people and eternal punishment for the same people–this is clearly an indication of the "passing under the rod" (Ezek. 20:37) of the people of Israel, of whom the believers of that nation, as well as the "sheep" (Matt. 25:32) of other nations who have believed the good news of the kingdom are made a part of that kingdom, versus the "children of the wicked one" who are sown into the field (Matt. 13:24–30).

Prophetic passages of the Old Testament make clear the fact that the nature of the messianic kingdom involves righteousness, peace, and extended life as a result of the lifting of the curse. First, righteousness is emphasized in such passages as Isaiah 52:1, which says in part speaking of the city of Zion, "for the uncircumcised and the unclean will no more come into you" (NASB). Isaiah 60:21 expresses it positively in this way, "Then all your people will be righteous; They will possess the land forever" (NASB). Perhaps the clearest expression of this is found in the passage which is quoted at the time of the Triumphal Entry in Matthew 21:5 which the prophet Isaiah was led to write, "Say to the daughter of Zion, 'Lo, your salvation comes; Behold His reward is with Him, and His recompense before Him.' And they will call them, 'The holy people, The redeemed of the Lord' " (Isa. 62:11–12 NASB). These prophetic passages, when taken in conjunction with the teaching of the Lord in Matthew, emphasize that those who enter the kingdom of heaven will be righteous.

An additional characteristic of this kingdom is that it is a kingdom of peace. Numerous Old Testament prophecies speak of this, but Isaiah 11:6–10 speaks of this in a way which indicates that the curse of sin will be removed during this time, because peace will not only be present amongst nations, but within the animal kingdom as well, allowing "the cow and the bear...[to]... graze; their young will lie down together; and the lion will eat straw like the ox" (Is. 11:7 NASB). Isaiah also is led to say, "No weapon that is formed against you shall prosper." (Isa. 54:10 NASB), and Zechariah 9:10 expresses it in this way, "And the bow of war will be cut off. And He will speak peace to the nations" (NASB).

It is important to note, since the objection is often made with regard to these passages dealing with the nature of the millennium, that they are speaking of the eternal kingdom following the establishing of the new heaven and new earth. That Isaiah makes a clear distinction which answers this concern. In Isaiah 65:17,

Isaiah begins a discourse with the phrase, "For behold I create new heavens and a new earth ... " (NASB) which would seem to imply that the discussion which immediately follows is speaking of that time. But notice that in the verses immediately following, which describe Jerusalem, that a "youth will die at the age of one hundred ... " (Isa. 65:20 NASB). Clearly, the fact that sorrow and crying are not present make it much like the coming mew Jerusalem, but in that city "there shall no longer be any death..." (Rev. 21:3 NASB) the apostle John tells us. The effects of the curse are removed in the millennial kingdom, but death is still present, as will be the sin nature, since Satan, upon his release will be able to "deceive the nations ... " (Rev. 20:8).

The **source of the millennial kingdom** is clearly God, through the Second Person of the Trinity. The prophet Daniel, in describing this event says:

> *"And behold, with the clouds of heaven One like a Son of Man was coming, And He came up to the Ancient of Days And was presented before Him. And to Him was given dominion, Glory and a Kingdom, That all the peoples, nations, and men of every language Might serve Him"* (Dan. 7:13–14 NASB).

The Lord Jesus, in His teaching regarding this same event, is recorded as saying in Matthew 24:30, "And they will see the SON OF MAN COMING ON THE CLOUDS OF THE SKY with power and great glory" (NASB).

When the prophets of the Old Testament, such as Zechariah, described the coming kingdom and its king by saying such things as, "And the Lord will be king over all the earth; in that day the Lord will be the only one, and His name the only one" (Zech. 14:9 NASB), it is clear that the fact that the nature of the kingdom is righteousness and peace is because the source of the kingdom is the Son of Righteousness.

The **purpose of the millennium** is primarily to fulfill the sovereign purpose of God. Any serious student of Scripture who is willing to approach the study of prophecy without preconceived concepts of ecclesiology must admit that a literal interpretation of prophecy requires a literal earthly kingdom. Even those who would desire to teach otherwise must accept this premise, as pointed out by Feinberg:

> *"Kuyper, in trying to refute chiliasm, makes admissions which substantially give his position away. In commenting on the passage (Rev. 20:1– 7), he notes: 'Reading this passage as if it were a literal description would not only tend to a belief in the Millennium but would settle the question of chiliasm for all who might be in doubt concerning the same .... If we take it for granted now, that these thousand years are to be taken literally, that these thousand years are still in the future, and that this resurrection was meant to be a bodily resurrection, why then we may say, that at least as far as Revelation 20 is concerned, the question is settled. Then we must admit that Revelation 20:1– 7 is a confession of chiliasm with all it contains."*[35]

What does the Scripture reveal regarding God's purpose? Clearly, prophetic Scripture indicates God's determination to fulfill His promises regarding Israel's future. It is interesting to note that the prophet Isaiah cites an event which is also cited by the Lord Jesus in speaking of the future of Israel. Isaiah says:

" *'For this is like the days of Noah to Me; When I swore that the waters of Noah should not flood the earth again, So I have sworn that I will not be angry with you, Nor will I rebuke you. For the mountains may be removed and the hills may shake, But My lovingkindness will not be removed from you, And My covenant of peace will not be shaken,' Says the Lord who has compassion on you"* *(Isa. 54:9–10 NASB).*

The Lord, of course, speaks of the days of Noah when He describes the time immediately preceding the "coming of the Son of Man" in glory in Matthew 24:37. God's promises are clear to the nation Israel and to the house of David, and so extensive throughout Scripture that it would involve a study in itself to begin to delineate them. The statement in Psalm 89:34 is perhaps the clearest representation of these promises, when Ehan the Ezrahite quotes the Almighty as saying, "My covenant I will not violate, Nor will I alter the utterance of My lips. Once I have sworn by My holiness; I will not lie to David. His descendants shall endure forever, And his throne as the sun before Me" (NASB).

The principle of God's continued purpose for the nation Israel is emphasized by the apostle Paul whose unique ministry was to make known the mystery of the Church, the body of Christ (Eph. 3:3). Paul, in the process of teaching the truth about the church, states very clearly that "God has not rejected His people whom He foreknew. Or do you not know what the Scripture says in the passage about Elijah, how he pleads with God against Israel" (Rom. 11:1 NASB), making it clear that God's people in this case is the nation Israel.

But perhaps the most important phase of the purpose of God in bringing about the Messianic kingdom of Christ on earth goes beyond His specific purpose for His people Israel, goes beyond His unfailing covenant with David, with Abraham, and with Israel, and goes beyond any specific promise to any individual, to the purpose of God throughout the history of the earth.

What is God's purpose in the world? None of us of finite mind can ever hope to fathom God's mind and purpose. But He has revealed certain concepts, in addition to all the details of His individual dealings with men. These concepts are perhaps best summarized in two verses of Scripture. The apostle Paul, quoting the prophet Isaiah says this of the purpose of God: "As I live, says the Lord, every knee shall bow to Me, and every tongue shall give praise to God" (Rom. 14:11 NASB). Paul, under the inspiration of the Holy Spirit elaborates on this statement even further in his letter to the Philippians:

> *"Therefore also God highly exalted Him, and bestowed on Him the name which is above every name, that at the name of Jesus every knee should bow, of those who are in heaven, and on earth, and under the earth, and that every tongue should*

confess that Jesus Christ is Lord, to the glory of God the Father" (Phil. 2:9–10 NASB).

But there is one further detail of God's plan. What about those who do not, in their earthly life, confess Jesus as Lord? Can a just God condemn them to eternal punishment? Again, the apostle Paul, as recorded in Romans 3:19, says that the Law speaks to those who are under the Law, "that every mouth may be stopped and all the world may become guilty before God" (NASB). What does this mean?

Let us take time to consider the unbeliever, who, at the close of time stands before the great white throne, as recorded in Revelation 20:11. Suppose that, as this individual stands before the bar of God and is asked to enter his plea, guilty or not guilty, he enters a plea of not guilty. When asked how he can do that, he replies that if he had not had a sin nature he would have been obedient to God's Law. God in justice can say, "No, I have already proven that man cannot obey, though he is created in innocence."

But the accused goes on then to say that if he had only had something to remind him of the distinction between good and evil, he would have always done good. God in justice can say, "No, I gave you a conscience, and you did not follow it when it reminded you of good and evil." But the accused goes on to say, but if there had been someone with authority to punish him when he did wrong, he would have obeyed, and of course God replies, "I gave that authority to human government, and you still lived in sin." The accused then has the audacity to say that if God had just written down what he was to do, he would have said, "All that the Lord hath spoken, we will do" (Ex. 24:3), and of course God need not reply to this, because as the accused speaks, his own words accuse him.

But then suppose that God speaks, and that He says that not only do you stand accused because of what has been said so far, but beyond this in matchless grace I loved you so much that I sent My Son, "that whosoever believeth in Him should not perish, but have everlasting life" (John 3:16). Perhaps God then goes on to say to the accused that when he would not believe even when God offered eternal life freely, God then established His Son as King over the earth, that He might rule with a "rod of iron" and enforce peace and righteousness in the earth. In spite of this, God goes on to say, mankind "repented not of their murders, their sorceries nor of their immorality nor of their thefts" (Rev. 9:21 NASB).

Now all of this is mere illustration, but the question is, How can a God who by His nature, by His very attributes, is infinitely just condemn one who does not believe? That can only be done after God has offered every opportunity so that in infinite justice "every mouth will be stopped and all the world will become guilty before God" (Rom. 3:19). Obviously, God will not need to go through these steps with the accused, because His holiness and justice will be apparent because He has thus dealt with man throughout history and in the light of that holiness, sin will be apparent as well, and the mouths will be stopped before they even open!

God's sovereign purpose to glorify His Son, and to make His holiness and justice known in His infinite judgments is the reason that there must be a literal earthly kingdom of the Messiah on earth. God has declared His purpose to do this, and we may have confidence in His Word. Praise His name!

APPENDIX

The following question is invariably asked in conjunction with this study. For this reason it is included as an addendum: WILL THE CHURCH GO THROUGH THE TRIBULATION?

In answer to this question, there is perhaps a more important question that the reader must deal with first, and that is this: What difference does it make? Or why should one waste their time worrying about it? Aren't there more important things to study? If the desire is merely to satisfy the curiosity of an idle mind, then the question is not significant. But, on the other hand, if the desire is to be guided into those principles which will be useful in practical daily Christian life, which is the ultimate purpose of all Christian doctrine, then the question is valuable and should be studied. With this precaution to keep in mind, let us proceed.

The first question that can be answered, since there can be a definitive answer to the question of the church and the tribulation, is this: Can I trust God's promises? It can be stated unequivocally that God has promised that the believer can expect to be delivered from judgment, (John 5:24), and to be delivered from "wrath" (1 Thess. 1:10). (See discussion of Philadelphia church in chapter seven).

Secondly, in order to answer the question of whether or not the Church will go through the tribulation, one must ask, who is the Church? Is it an organization which needs to be "purified," or is it individuals who are believers in the Lord Jesus Christ? If it is individuals, the criteria for fellowship and inclusion in the body is whether or not a person is a believer. If it is an organization, the question that each of us must ask ourselves, are we sure we have examined all the possible options and are we sure we are in the right organization?

Certainly this question is not a critical one for most evangelical Christians, and yet it strikes to the heart of the historical problem, because, if the Church is an organization, if it is the agency through which the kingdom on earth will be established, it clearly needs purification, and therefore will go through the Tribulation. The reader should examine carefully any arguments that have been read or studied which show that the Church will go through the Tribulation to determine if this is the basis for the decision. Much of the basis, historically, for the position which would put the Church through the Tribulation, comes from a lack of distinction between the Church as an organism, the body of Christ, or an organization, be it Roman Catholic, Eastern Orthodox, Reformed, Lutheran, or whatever. It is clear that the New Testament makes distinction between these, and carefully defines the means by which one becomes a part of the Church through personal faith in the Lord Jesus Christ.

Third, to answer the question one must also ask, is the tribulation still ahead? For some, this may seem a strange question, but there is an eschatological position which believes that the Tribulation took place immediately after Christ's ascension. Note that the Lord Jesus, in response to the question of the disciples, "When shall these things be," indicates that the time of tribulation will occur and that immediately after those days, the Son of Man will come. What does the word immediately indicate? This word is used several times in the book of Matthew as well as elsewhere in the Gospels. Some of these occurrences are:

1 Matthew 8:7 - Immediately his leprosy was cleansed
2 Matthew 20:34 - Immediately their eyes received their sight.
3 Mark 1:31 - Immediately (understood in English but shown in Greek) the fever left her.
4 Mark 1:42 - Immediately the leprosy left him.
5 Mark 6:27 - Immediately the king sent an executioner.

It would seem apparent from these usages, that the one event follows the other, as we understand the word in English, immediately, and thus the tribulation immediately precedes the Second Coming of the Son of Man to establish His throne.

Fourth, we should ask, is the tribulation to be any different from trials we have now? What will it be?

Again, some cite the quotation from our Lord in John 16:33 to indicate that tribulation is an ongoing thing for the believer. This is true, but notice that in Matthew 24:21 the Lord Himself is speaking and His words are that this time will be so great a time of tribulation that there is none like it before or since. Again, in Joel 2::2 "there has never been anything like it, nor will ever be again hereafter...." This time is described as a time of destruction in Joel 1:15–16, a time that will "come as destruction ... " and in Joel 2:12 as "a day of darkness and gloom ...."

It is further stated in Joel 2:32 that those who call on the name of the Lord will be saved. Saved in what way? Saved from destruction, quite literally, from the destructive judgment that will be poured out at that time. This is particularly apparent when one realizes further that this time is described as a time of judgment and purging for Israel in such prophecies as Ezekiel 20:33–44 and Zechariah 13:8–14:8.

In summary, and in relation to what we have said above, the prophetic portions also indicate that the time of tribulation will culminate with the return of Christ to the earth as indicated in Zechariah 14:4 (Where will He return to? The Mount of Olives.) and Acts 1:11–12 (Where did He go from? The Mount of Olives). Will the Church (we as believers) be here?

A. The Lord Jesus Himself said that there will be no judgment for believers John 5:24.

B. Believers do not *dwell* on the Earth.

1 Philippians 3:20 says that "our citizenship is in heaven."

2 The term "dwell" is never used of believers in the Lord Jesus Christ in the New Testament. It is a term which means more than "live" as we think of it. The word is in Col 2:9 "in Him all the fulness of Deity dwells in human form."

3 The word dwell is used of those who are not believers in Rev 3:10, 13:8, 14:6,

C. First Thessalonians 4:13–18 and 5:6 and 9 seems to be clearly contrasted with 1 Thess. 5:3, 10 in that one speaks clearly of "we" and "us" as those believers to whom the epistle is directed, while the other speaks of "they" and "them" as those who dwell on the Earth. Note that this is speaking of the period of time referred to as the "Day of the Lord." Remember the passages in Joel where the time known as the "Day of the Lord" is referred to as a time of judgment for Israel? (See Joel 1:15 as an example).

D. Remember the passages in Matthew 13.

1 The measures of meal had to be "thrashed" and "ground, the chaff removed or "purged." Certainly this is the picture of the nation Israel undergoing thrashing and purging under the hand of God during this time of Tribulation.

2 The "treasure" is purchased with the field, indicating that its place is in the world–Israel is God's earthly people.

3 The "pearl" is purchased "out of the field" (*exagorazo*) "redeemed," which is spoken of over and over in the New Testament of the Church (1 Peter 1:18–19) indicating to set free after having been purchased in the Forum, the slave market. Praise God, we have been redeemed!

THE *LAST* TRUMPET?

Throughout the centuries, the debate has gone on and continues to this very day. The question of the Lord's return for His Church is a question that it seems difficult to resolve. Many theologians have dismissed any discussion of the matter, citing the philosophy that it is not important to "major on the minors." But, is that truth which is called in Scripture the "Blessed Hope" a minor truth? The apostle John reminds the readers of his epistle that "every man that hath this hope in him purifieth himself, even as he is pure" (1 John 3:3). Does the knowledge of the timing of Christ's return make us more effective in our Christian life? It seems that the teaching of this verse would indicate that.

There were different shapes of shofar, depending on the type of ram from which they were taken, as well as his age and development

As is often the case in the process of interpreting and "handling accurately" the Word of God, the answer to this question does not lie in what theologians throughout the centuries have speculated. It lies in the careful reading and understanding of the phrase which is the title of this treatise. As one who grew up under the teaching of a godly pastor, my father, and was exposed each year to one or more week-long series conducted in the local church by such men of God as Dr. Harry Ironside, Dr. Louis T. Talbot, Dr. Charles L. Feinberg,

Dr. John Walvoord, Dr. J. Elwood Evans, and Dr. J. Vernon McGee (to name just a few) I learned at an early age from these great men that it mattered not what man said, but what God's Word said.

And so, the question that must be answered is this: What is the significance of the term "last" in the passage in 1 Corinthians 15:51–52 which says, "Behold, I tell you a mystery, we shall not all sleep, but we shall all be changed, in a moment, in the twinkling of an eye, at the last trumpet; for the trumpet will sound, and the dead will be raised imperishable, and we shall be changed" (NASV).

What is the last trumpet? When did the first one sound? How many have sounded since then? How will one know it is the last one? All of these questions are not readily answered by a New Testament believer, especially one who is a Gentile and has little or no knowledge and tradition in Judaism. But the apostle Paul, the author of these words, through the guidance of the Holy Spirit, was steeped in the Jewish tradition. He was educated at the feet of Gamaliel, he tells us (Acts 22:3), who was a "doctor of the law, had in reputation among all the people" (Acts 5:34), one who knew the traditions and teachings of the Old Testament and the Jewish faith.

We understand from the tradition of the rabbis, that there are three significant "trumpets" or blowing of the shofar, or ram's horn, in the Scripture. The first trumpet sounds in Exodus 19:16 at the giving of the Law. Jewish tradition holds that the trumpet was heard throughout the inhabited earth and that the giving of the Ten Commandments was also heard in the 70 languages of the then-known earth (thus, the Lord sent out the 70; Luke 10). The great trumpet, according to Jewish tradition, is the one that will sound at the coronation of the Messiah (Rev. 11:15) when Israel is restored to her place at the head of the nations. The last trumpet, the one that is the focus of our attention, according to Jewish tradition, sounds at the beginning of the Day of the Lord when God begins His regathering of the nation of Israel from their dispersion amongst the nations. It is that shofar which is of significance in this study. But, apart from Jewish tradition, there must be a scriptural basis for Paul's reference to the "last trump" and we must be able to verify that time in more than Jewish tradition or we will fall into the same pit that those who have based it on Christian tradition have fallen.

The teaching of the Old Testament involves two distinct types of trumpets. The silver trumpets (*chatzotzerah*) that were made to be a part of the tabernacle worship (Numbers 10), and the *shofarim* (plural form of *shofar*), or ram's horns, which were used to announce the beginning of festivals, were used to sound an alarm related to the marching order of Israel, a call to assemble, or a call to muster troops for war, to warn of danger (Ezek. 33:1–7) and for signals in the midst of battle (see Numbers 10:5–9). They were also blown at a coronation and thus the tradition of the great trumpet at the crowning of the Messiah.

But having looked at the general teaching regarding the use of the shofarim in the Old Testament, is there teaching which will help us to determine when the last trumpet will sound? One of the key times when the shofar was also blown was to announce the beginning of festivals. There is one additional time for which Israel is given instruction regarding the blowing of the shofar, the ram's horn trumpet. That instruction is given in Leviticus 25 in relation to the year of jubilee. On the Day of Atonement in the forty-ninth year, the shofar was to be blown and the fiftieth year was to be a sabbatical year for the land and a year of release. The instructions make it clear that all debts were to be forgiven in the land of Israel "to all its inhabitants" (Lev 25:10).

The instructions regarding this year of jubilee indicate that "On that year of jubilee each of you shall return to his own property" (Lev. 25:13). This instruction was given to Moses and was to be applied, as the second verse of the twenty-fifth chapter of Leviticus indicates, after the sons of Israel had come into the Promised Land and the land had been divided for the inheritance of each tribe and family. Thus, as promised to Abraham, God's covenant with him was to be an everlasting covenant which guaranteed to him and to his descendants an eternal inheritance in the land which God promised to him (Gen. 12:1, 15:18–21).

It is worthy of note at this point, given the pattern of history in many societies which discriminate against women, that the daughters of Zelophehad were guaranteed an inheritance based upon their father's right, not related to their husband's so long as they married within the extended tribal family, so that the inheritance would remain in the family (Num 27:1–

7; 36:6), surely an evidence of God's recognition of women as persons of value to him, and contrary to the traditions of men which for centuries treated women as mere property.

So, at every forty-ninth year, counting in increments of fifty, the ram's horn was blown and Israel returned to their inheritance. What happened? The prophets, particularly Ezekiel, report that the clear instructions given in Exodus 31:13 & 17 regarding the keeping of the Sabbaths by the nation Israel were not being observed. In Ezekiel 20:20, the Lord reviews with Ezekiel the fact that the Sabbaths were a sign of the covenant between Israel and the Lord and when those Sabbaths were not observed God accused them of despising His statutes and polluting His Sabbaths (Ezek. 20:24). In addition, Jeremiah specifically cites the sabbatical years and Israel's disobedience in regard to them as a reason for their dispersion (Jer. 34:8, 13–14).

As a practical matter, what sign has the Lord given to New Testament believers to show that we are His people? John 13:35 says this, "By this shall all men know that ye are my disciples, if ye have love one to another." What a sobering thought. Are we like Israel? As they abandoned the observance of the Sabbath, have we lost sight of what love for one another really means? Do we admonish and encourage one another? Do we remind one another of the truth and seek to restore those who have stumbled? Or do we blithely assume that is "their business" and take no care for our brother?

May God grant that we will learn from the example of Israel which God has given to us for our learning (1 Cor. 10:11).

So, it is a given fact that the jubilee shofar, if we can identify it as such, has not sounded in Israel for many centuries because of their disobedience and dispersion. Will it sound again? The prophet Isaiah, in chapter 27, utters these significant words, "And it will come about in that day, that the Lord will begin his threshing from the flowing stream of the Euphrates to the brook of Egypt; and you will be gathered up one by one, O sons of Israel. It will come about in that day that a great trumpet will be blown; and those who were perishing in the land of Assyria and who were scattered in the land of Egypt will come and worship the Lord in the holy mountain at Jerusalem" (Isa. 27:12–13). This is the day that signifies the beginning of the regathering of Israel under God's hand. This regathering is spoken of in Ezekiel 20 in the passage that pronounced judgment for profaning the Sabbaths, and the prophet indicates that Israel will be gathered "face to face" (Ezek. 27:35) and they will "pass under the rod" (27:37), indicating that the judgment is to be an individual gathering, as the prophet Isaiah in the passage cited above indicated, in the same way that the shepherd separated his individual sheep from the sheep from other flocks.

In the time of the writing of the testaments, after Israel was in the land, it was customary to establish a town sheepfold where the sheep could be housed overnight under the care of an hireling. When the shepherd came in the morning for his sheep, he would stand at the opening in the rock wall, the gate, and call his sheep. He would hold his rod over the opening, and when a sheep who was not one of his flock came, he would lower his rod and not allow it to exit the fold. Thus, all the sheep that were his "passed under the rod." This is the picture of what God will do with and for Israel during the "time of Jacob's trouble," when God winnow's, or threshes, Israel and judges the nations, that seven-year period know as Daniel's seventieth week (Dan. 9:24ff).

Does the trumpet sound at the beginning of that week? Does the beginning of that "week" have a particular distinction? The prophet Joel, in the second chapter of his prophecy, marks the sounding of an alarm, a shofar, as the ushering in of the Day of the Lord. It is described by Joel as a time of judgment and gloom, as well as a time of ultimate preservation of Israel and blessing upon them. Joel challenges Israel to return to the Lord and promises God's future blessing upon them when that takes place. Clearly, that has not yet happened, in spite of the fact that a partial "regathering" of Judah has occurred, the nation Israel remains in exile. But it will happen when the trumpet blows. The prophet Zephaniah also speaks of the blowing of the trumpet as a part of judgment and destruction and the gathering together of Israel for purging and blessing (Zeph. 1:16).

One of the teachings which has caused great confusion regarding the return of the Lord is whether or not there is a future for Israel. The Church of the Dark Ages promulgated the concept, beginning with Augustine, that God was done with Israel and that all of the promises of God to Israel were to be fulfilled in the church. Such teaching denies the clear teaching of Scripture. There are many illustrations which make this clear, but perhaps the easiest with which to draw the distinction is the prophecy of Zechariah regarding the physical return of Christ to establish His earthly kingdom. That prophecy says this, "And in that day His feet will stand on the Mount of Olives … " (Zech. 14:4a). The amillenialist, that is, the one who does not believe in a literal earthly kingdom of Christ as promised to Israel, makes the statement of this verse "symbolic". Hence, it is not a specific day that this prophecy is to be fulfilled, it is not the actual feet of the Messiah, and it is not literally the Mount of Olives.

The question that must be asked at that point is, Was Mary a *virgin* (Isa. 7:14)? The answer given by those who promulgate this "symbolism" is, well of course she was. But the fact is that the proper reading of the prophecy in Hebrew is not as specific as Zechariah's prophecy. Those who are students of the Hebrew language realize that there is no specific word for virgin in Hebrew and thus the clarity and meaning of the verse must come from its interpretation recorded in the New Testament, written in a language which has a very specific word, by God's sovereign purpose, which quotes the prophecy of Isaiah 7:14 as saying, "Behold, the virgin shall be with child … "(Matt. 1:23a). Even though the Scripture, like any language, may use symbolism, it is clear from the language and usage that this is what is being done. Dr. Louis T. Talbot used to say, "When the plain sense makes common sense, seek no other sense." That is an excellent guideline for the student of hermeneutics. It is also important to examine parallel passages of Scripture which speak on the same subject.

With that in mind, we move briefly to the consideration of the great trumpet. In view of the prophecy of Zechariah regarding the literal kingdom to be established by the Messiah here on the Earth, it is significant to note that the prophecy of our Lord Jesus, who certainly would be considered an authority of future events, describes the coming of the Son of Man as being heralded by a "great trumpet" (Matt. 24:31). Again, a citation regarding a particular shofar by an individual acquainted with Jewish custom and tradition, by the One who is the final authority on Scriptural interpretation.

Having thus looked at these trumpets, what significance does the last trumpet have for the Church? First, it marks a point in relation to other prophetic events that gives definition to time. The Last Trumpet, as we have seen, is blown at the beginning of the time when God begins to regather Israel. That is not in the middle of the seventieth week of Daniel, nor is it at the end. It is at the beginning of that week as evidenced by the reference in Revelation 7 to the sealing of the 144,000, representatives from each of the twelve tribes of Israel at the beginning of the tribulation.

It is important to note at this point something which is learned by every police officer who is interviewing witnesses to an event. It is almost impossible to recount what is seen in absolute chronological order.

In order to present a logical account of an event, each phase is usually completed by a witness and then one backs up to revisit another aspect of the event. For instance, a witness reviewing the events of an accident at an intersection where vehicles approaching from perpendicular routes will usually recall the route of one vehicle from the approach to the intersection to the point of impact, and then recount the route and actions of the other vehicle and driver in attempting to avoid the accident. If the account was taken step by step in absolute chronological order it, would be so disjointed as to be difficult to follow.

This is the way the apostle John recounts his vision of events in Revelation. He completes what he sees in relation to one aspect of his vision before beginning another aspect of the vision, and thus may back up chronologically in order to give a complete picture. One clear example of this is a comparison of Revelation chapter fourteen, which proceeds through a series of events to culminate with the battle of Armageddon. Later, in chapter nineteen, it also proceeds in a similar manner with a different perspective of events to the same battle of Armageddon. Are there two battles? Of course not. It is merely a logical progression through John's visions of all the details that he sees which relate to the prophetic future that was revealed to him. This is, in part, a reason for the confusion that relates, at times, to the timing of various events and it is important to "stand back and see the big picture."

So, there will come a day when Israel will be regathered and in accordance with God's covenant with

Abraham will inherit the land promised to him and his descendants through Isaac. Jeremiah 3:15–18 speaks of this time as a time of restoration to God's blessing, a time of peace, and a time of permanent inheritance. Since it will be such a time, there will be no indebtedness because of God's blessing on the fruitfulness of the land. There will be no loss of inheritance and thus no need for a year of jubilee because the Lord will, having purified Israel and established His authority, keep them at peace and in safety, as prophesied in Jeremiah 30:7ff. That final jubilee, which will at one and the same time be an "alarm" to call Israel to assemble, will be the last trumpet for the purpose of jubilee because their inheritance will from thenceforth be secure. It will be the last call to assemble, because they will not again march, nor war, nor have any cause for alarm, because they will be at peace (Jer. 31:31–33). The only trumpet they will hear following the last trumpet will be the great trumpet of the coronation of the king, as noted above.

What other people are God's people besides Israel? The Church is God's heavenly people. When God calls His people to return to their inheritance, when God calls to gather His people to dwell in peace, when God calls His people to be free from alarm, where will be the inheritance of the Church? Of course, the student of Scripture immediately calls to mind the words of the apostle Paul in Philippians 3:20, "For our citizenship is in heaven; from whence also we look for the Savior, the Lord Jesus Christ." This is promised to be "an inheritance incorruptible, and undefiled, and that fadeth not away, reserved in heaven for you" (1 Peter

1:4). This is the Blessed Hope, the source of "exceeding joy" (Jude 1:24), and the promise of eternal blessing in His presence. This return is imminent in every sense of the word.

And so, given the certainty of the events surrounding the last trumpet in relation to Israel, and given the nature of those events in relation to regathering, winnowing, preserving of the testimony of the 144,000, who at this point are still under judicial blindness and will not have that blindness removed until the Church is called to their inheritance (Romans 11:25), those who promulgate a mid-tribulation view, or a pre-wrath view, or a post-tribulation view fail to note this important passage in Romans. They argue that even though the Church did not appear in any of Daniel's sixty-nine weeks, that there is nothing in Scripture to separate the Church from Israel in the seventieth week!

The clear teaching of Paul in the New Testament is the distinction between Israel and the Church. God's judgment of Israel because of their rejection of their Messiah, and His "setting aside" of Israel in order to manifest His grace to the Gentiles, is an important element in the New Testament revelation of the mystery of the Church, a mystery not previously revealed (Eph 1:9, 3:3ff, 5:32) and which is taught and revealed primarily, not in the Gospels or prior to the close of the book of Acts except in transitional form.

One of the dangers to every student of scriptural hermeneutics is the danger of seeking church doctrine in the Gospels or the transitional book of Acts. It is irrevocably true that "all Scripture … is profitable" but it must also be handled accurately in relation to its interpretation for those to whom it is specifically directed. When the 144,000 and the rest of Israel and Judah have the judicial blindness removed after the rapture of the Church, the Scripture tells that they will "look upon me whom they have pierced" (Zech. 12:10). It is of great importance to note that this blindness will not be removed until "the fulness of the Gentiles be come in: and thus all Israel will be saved" (Rom. 11:25). Clearly, God is now done with "taking from among the Gentiles a people for His name" (Acts 15:14) … His dealing with the Church is finished because the "fullness of the Gentiles" has come in. James goes on to make a statement of great significance, conspicuously overlooked by those of the mid–tribulation rapture, pre–wrath, and post-trib position. James' statement is, "After this I will return … " (Acts 15:15ff). There is a distinct line drawn between God's dealing with the Gentiles and with Israel as James elucidates it for us.

At that point, there is also a significant question that one may propose. If Israel begins to realize that Jesus is their Messiah, as God removes their blindness and challenges them to preach the "gospel of the kingdom," and they realize that perhaps there is a New Testament which teaches the truth about that Messiah, where will they begin to read. Most people begin an unfamiliar book at the beginning. God, in His sovereign plan and purpose, has seen fit to preserve the New Testament, not in the chronological order of its writing, but with Matthew, the gospel of the kingdom and the king, as the first book in the New Testament. It is here that Israel will begin to learn that gospel and will be challenged, as the disciples and the seventy were, to go "and make disciples of all the nations" (Matt. 28:19). Clearly, they will not have that anointing of the Spirit spoken of by the prophet Joel (2:28) until the judicial blindness has been removed, because "the entrance of Thy Word giveth light" (Psa. 119:130). That, once again a reminder of what Paul says, will not occur until the "fullness of the Gentiles be come in" (Rom. 11:25) and God is through dealing with the Gentiles, and in contrast to Acts 28:28 where the gospel is to go to the Gentiles, God now returns, as James indicated in Acts 15:16, quoting the prophet Amos, that God's promise is that "after this I will return and I will rebuild" the nation of Israel. After what? After God's dealing with the Church, apart from the Law and through the gospel of His grace. It is clear from even a cursory reading of such passages that there is a clear time frame for God's dealing with the Church which is not coupled in any way with His dealing with Israel. His return to dealing with Israel clearly, again in the words of James is "after this."

So, the last trumpet is sounded as a signal to all of God's people. Paul, knowing the promise to the Jews and the designation by Jewish teachers of that trumpet because it is the final signal to Israel apart from the coronation of their Messiah, calls it by that name in speaking to the Church. We, as Gentiles, have not followed the example of the Bereans and searched the Scripture to determine what significance was attached to the label Paul, by the inspiration of the Holy Spirit, gave to that signal of our translation into the immortal sphere. Only God knows how many hours of effective ministry may have been lost through disputing the time of Christ's return. It is imminent, clearly, as the Thessalonians were taught. It maintains the distinction between the Church and Israel, as has often been misinterpreted. It remains the Blessed Hope because God "has not appointed us to wrath but to obtain salvation by our Lord Jesus Christ" (1 Thess. 5:9).

To attempt to promulgate the concept that the wrath portion of the tribulation is only a small portion of time at the end flies in the face of the prophet's warning to Israel. The blowing of the trumpet, the alarm spoken of by Joel is not merely background music for Israel's return to the land! It is an alarm of judgment and winnowing, threshing, of Israel. That picture of the owner is cited by John the Baptist in Matthew 3:12 and is not a picture of gentle nurture, but a true picture of the process of removing the wheat from the chaff, through beating and fanning, or walking over repeatedly and fanning into the wind and allowing the chaff to blow away. The Time of Jacob's trouble begins with the trumpet.

The four horsemen of the Apocalypse are not Paul Revere; they are the harbingers of death and destruction. They are not messengers but delivery persons! The fifth seal of Revelation 6 includes a picture of those who have already been martyred because they have repented, believing that the kingdom of heaven is at hand. Given the progression of the subsequent chapters of Revelation and the time frame mentioned in relation to the progression of the first three and one half years, the breaking of the covenant with Israel at the middle of that time, all of which is preceded by famine, pestilence on the Earth and by Israel being separated as the five wise and five foolish virgins pictured by the Lord in Matthew 25, all of this indicates a time which we, certainly those of us living in peace in the Western world, would probably consider judgment!

May God enable us to make clear distinction between Israel's future and the future of the Church, the body of Christ. May He enable us to be clear in our message of the Blessed Hope, so that we can "comfort one another with these words" (1 Thess. 4:18).

BIBLIOGRAPHY

A. BOOKS

Anderson, Sir Robert, *The Coming Prince*. Grand Rapids: Kregel Publications, reprint of the 10th edition, 1983.

Buksbazen, Victor. *The Gospel in the Feasts of Israel*. St. Louis: Midwest Messianic Center, 1965.

Chafer, Lewis Sperry. *The Kingdom in History and Prophecy*. Chicago: The Bible Institute Colportage Ass'n., 1936.

Clouse, Robert G. ed. *The Meaning of the Millennium*. Downers Grove, Illinois: InterVarsity Press, 1977.

Feinberg, Charles L. *Premillennialism or Amillennialism?* Wheaton: Van Kampen Press, 1954.

Good, Joseph. *Rosh HaShanah and the Messianic Kingdom to Come*. Port Arthur, Texas: Hatikva Ministries, 1989

Graham, Billy. *Approaching Hoofbeats, The Four Horsemen of the Apocalypse.* Minneapolis: Grason, 1983.

Grant, F. W. *The Lessons of the Ages.* New York: Loizeaux Brothers, Publishers.

Ironside, Harry A. *Lectures on Daniel the Prophet.* New York: Loizeaux Brothers, Publishers

Lockyer, Herbert. *All the Parables of the Bible.* Grand Rapids: Zondervan Publishing House, 1963.

MacArthur, John F. Jr. *The Gospel According to Jesus.* Grand Rapids: Zondervan Publishing House, 1988.

Ockenga, Harold J. *The Church in God.* Westwood, New Jersey: Gleming H. Revell Co., 1956.

Ottman, Ford C. *Imperialism and Christ.* New York: Charles C. Cook, 1912.

Pentecost, J. Dwight. *Things to Come.* Grand Rapids: Zondervan Publishing House, 1958.

Ryrie, Charles Caldwell. *The Basis of the Premillennial Faith.* New York: Loizeaux Brothers, 1953.

_____. *Revelation.* Chicago: Moody Press, 1968.

Thiessen, Henry Clarence. *Introductory Lectures in Systematic Theology*. Grand Rapids: Wm. B. Eerdmans Publishing Co., 1961.

Wilson, William. *Wilson's Old Testament Word Studies*. McLean, VA: MacDonald Publishing Co.

B. BOOKS: MULTIPLE VOLUME WORKS

Chafer, Lewis Sperry. *Systematic Theology* 8 vols. Dallas: Dallas Seminary Press, 1947.

Nicoll, W. Robertson, ed. *The Expositor's Greek Testament* 5 vols. Grand Rapids: Wm. B. Eerdmans Publishing Co.

C. DICTIONARIES, CONCORDANCES AND LEXICONS

Thayer, Joseph Henry. *Thayer's Greek–English Lexicon of the New Testament*. Marshallton, Delaware: The National Foundation for Christian Education, reprint of 1885 edition.

Thomas, Robert L. ed. *New American Standard Exhaustive Concordance of the Bible, Hebrew–Aramaic–Greek Dictionaries* Nashville: Holman, 1981.

Vine, W.E. *A Comprehensive Dictionary of the Original Greek Words with their Precise Meanings for English Readers*. McLean, VA: MacDonald Publishing Co.

Young, Robert. *Young's Analytical Concordance.* Grand Rapids: Associated Publishers and Authors Inc.

D. BIBLES

Aland, Kurt et al. ed. *The Greek New Testament.* Stuttgart, West Germany: Wurttemberg Bible Society, 1966

Scofield, Cyrus Ingerson, ed. *New Scofield Study Bible/New American Standard.* New York: Oxford University Press, 1988.

_____. *The Scofield Reference Bible.* New York: Oxford University Press, 1945.

E. UNPUBLISHED MATERIAL

Eadie, Clarence. "Biblical Literature." Class lectures given at the University of Redlands, Redlands, California. June, 1965.

END NOTES

1   Lewis Sperry Chafer, *Systematic Theology: Prolegomena, Bibliology, Theology Proper*, vol. 1, (Dallas: Dallas Seminary Press, 1947), 114.

2   Ibid.

3   "The Kingdom of God" is (a) the sphere of God's rule, Ps. 22:28; 145:13; Dan. 4:25; Luke 1:52; Rom 13:1,2. Since, however, this earth is the scene of universal rebellion against God, eg, Luke 4:5,6; I John 5:19; Rev. 11:5–18, the Kingdom of God is (b) the sphere in which, at any given time, His rule is acknowledged. God has not relinquished His sovereignty in the face of rebellion, demoniac and human, but has declared His purpose to establish it, Dan. 2:44; 7:14; I Cor. 15:24,25. Meantime, seeking willing obedience, He gave His law to a nation and appointed kings to administer His Kingdom over it, 1 Chron. 28:5. Israel, however, though

declaring still a nominal allegiance shared in the common rebellion, Isa. 1:2–4, and, after they had rejected the Son of God, John 1:11 (cp Matt. 21:33–43), were "cast away," Rom. 11:15, 20, 25. Henceforth God calls upon men everywhere, without distinction of race or nationality, to submit voluntarily to His rule. Thus, speaking generally, references to the kingdom fall into two classes, the first, in which it is viewed as present and involving suffering for those who enter it, II Thess. 1:5; the second, in which it is viewed as future and is associated with reward, Matt. 25:34, and glory, 13:43. See also Acts 14:22." W.E. Vine, *A Comprehensive Dictionary of the Original Greek Words with their Precise Meanings for English Readers*, (McLean, Virginia: MacDonald Publishing), 634.

4   Chafer, op. cit., 119.

5   Harry A. Ironside, *Lectures on Daniel the Prophet*, (New York: Loizeaux Brothers), 26.

6   Ibid.

7   Sir Robert Anderson, *The Coming Prince*, (Grand Rapids: Kregel reprint of the tenth edition, 1983), 127.

8   Ibid.

9   Ibid., 128.

10 Vine, op.cit., 635.

11 Revelation 1:1, Kurt Aland et al, ed, *The Greek New Testament*, (New York: American Bible Society, 1966), 836.

12 Charles C. Ryrie, *Revelation* (Chicago: Moody Press, 1968), 21.

13 Cyrus I. Scofield, ed, Scofield Reference Bible (New York: Oxford University Press, 1969), note at Revelation 1:20.

14 Ibid.

15 Ibid.

16 Ibid.

17 Ibid.

18 Ibid.

19 Ibid.

20 Revelation 3:10, Aland ed, op. cit., 844.

21 Aland, ed, op cit. at Scripture references indicated.

22 Vine, op. cit., 962.

23 Joseph Good, *Rosh HaShanah and the Messianic Kingdom to Come*, (Port Arthur, Texas: Hatikva Ministries, 1989), 48.

24 Good, op.cit., 50.

25 Anderson, op. cit., 83–85.

26 Harry A. Ironside, "Lectures on the Revelation," 287.95 as quoted in J. Dwight Pentecost, *Things to*

Come, (Grand Rapids: Zondervan Publishing, 1958), 365–367.

27 Ibid.

28 Ibid.

29 Good, op. cit., 68–69.

30 Charles L. Feinberg, *Premillennialism or Amillennialism?*, (Wheaton: Van Kampen Press, 1954), 169.

31 Thayer, op. cit., 360.

32 Ibid., 101

33 Thayer, op. cit., 158.

34 Clarence Eady, "Biblical Introduction", class notes taken at University of Redlands. 1965.

35 Charles L. Feinberg, *PreMillennialism or Amillennialism?*, (Wheaton, Illinois: Van Kampen Press, 1954), 169, quoting A. Kuyper, Chiliasm, 9.

www.ingramcontent.com/pod-product-compliance
Lightning Source LLC
LaVergne TN
LVHW011327080426
835513LV00006B/235